your mission to become a man

By Lee Burns and Braxton Brady

Table of Contents

Introduction   5

1   Buckle Up   7

2   On Course Or Off Course?   13

3   Flight Pattern   25

4   Who Is Going To Be Your Wing Man?   45

5   Cabin Pressure   55

6   Potential Crash Landing   71

7   Girls Like Guys In Uniform   91

8   Afterburners On!   105

9   Red Flags   125

10 Call Signs And Crew Chiefs   137

11 Flight School   153

12 Medals Of Honor   167

13 Final Tune Up   183

Appendix   192

Praise for **Flight Plan***:*

I regret that each young man coming into my tutelage did not have his adolescence shaped by *Flight Plan*. This superb resource, with its Christian underpinnings, frank explanations, and practical solutions, provides a wonderful road map for boys who are approaching the tough and complex challenges presented by life today.

Flight Plan should be a primary text for every boy trying to figure out how to become a man.

*– **B. B. Bell***
Four Star General, U.S. Army (Retired);
Former Commander, U.S. and Allied Forces, Korea

As a coach, parent, pastor and advocate for the healthy development of boys into men, *Flight Plan* is a terrific guide to help boys take the journey most men have not traveled. I found it accessible, extremely relevant and very practical. Anyone who has the privilege of working with young men will find this immeasurably helpful to develop the heart, mind and souls of young men. The added value is that any man who reads and implements this book you will find your concepts of masculinity challenged and changed.

*–**Joe Ehrman***
Former NFL player, author, coach and speaker;
Co-Founder, Building Men and Women For Others

As a therapist, every day I sit with boys and young men who are lost, hungry for relationship, and struggling. Young males in our culture are desperate for information, attention, and understanding.

Lee Burns and Braxton Brady have made having some vital conversations with the boys we love an easy and well-defined journey. These two men are wise, innovative, seasoned educators. They are also passionate, invested, accessible fathers. It is from both of those places that they chart the way for the rest of us.

I wouldn't suggest you get a copy of this book and read it with a boy you love, I would strongly recommend you do so.

*– **David Thomas***
Director of Counseling for Men and Boys, Daystar Counseling;
Author of Wild Things: The Art of Nurturing Boys

Introduction

Mission: an operation that is assigned by a higher headquarters

The B-17 Flying Fortress *"Memphis Belle"* was one of 12,750 B-17's built by the Boeing Aircraft Company during WWII. The Belle was the most famous because she was the first heavy bomber in Hitler's European war theatre to complete 25 combat missions and keep her entire crew alive. Morale was extremely low at this time because 80% of the bombers were shot down during the first three months of America's combat flights over Europe.

The Belle shot down eight enemy fighters, probably destroyed five others, and damaged at least a dozen more. She dropped more than 60 tons of bombs over Germany, France and Belgium. During her 25 missions she flew 148 hours, 50 minutes, and covered more than 20,000 combat miles. She is the only B-17 to have her own file in the Air Force Film Depository.

This plane was bullet-ridden and on five separate occasions had engines shot out and once came back with her tail nearly shot off. There was not one major injury to the crew members. The plane's mission was accomplished.

You are about to embark on a mission. It is one of the most important of your life. It is your mission to become a man. Over the next several years, you will experience the ups and downs of growing from boyhood into manhood. Make no mistake about it; this mission is not an easy one. The journey to becoming a godly man will force you to make some difficult decisions that will greatly impact your future.

You might be asking yourself, "How do I know what to do?" That is the purpose of this book. We want to help you along the way, giving you advice and helping you navigate through some of those difficult situations. This book will give you the "flight plan" for your mission.

We want you to take your time and read carefully. The information in this book is for you. We don't claim to have all the answers, but we know it will be a valuable resource to you. Before you begin your mission, we want to offer some suggestions:

- Read each chapter carefully (more than once if necessary).
- Underline, write notes in the margin and write down any questions you might have.
- Take your time and answer the discussion questions honestly.
- Discuss the book with your friends (it helps to have more than one opinion on something).
- Discuss each chapter with your father, mentor, coach or someone you respect (it is very important to discuss this with someone who has completed the mission).

Our hope is that this book encourages and challenges you each step of the way. Just like the *Memphis Belle*, you might experience some difficulty in the air. Don't give up. Arrival at the destination of godly manhood is well worth the flight!

Chapter 1

Buckle Up

Roger, liftoff, and the clock is started.

— Alan B. Shepard Jr., Astronaut

It was my fear that made me learn everything I could about my airplane and my emergency equipment, and kept me flying respectful of my machine and always alert in the cockpit.

— Chuck Yeager, General

The engines roar so loudly you can feel your whole body shake as the fighter jet accelerates down the short runway on the aircraft carrier in the middle of the Pacific Ocean. You can smell the burning fuel. Standing on the deck of the carrier, you can't even see the fighter pilot inside because his plane is racing by at such an incredible speed. You can, though, sense the power of the great plane and the intensity of the takeoff. Just seconds before, the jet was calmly stationed at the end of the carrier, along with a few other ones. But now, just seconds later, amidst burning fuel and an awesome display of speed, it's at the end of the runway and quickly airborne, racing up into the blue sky.

But where is the plane going?

Like the fighter jet, you are also about to accelerate down a short runway and take off on a great adventure with many possible missions and destinations. During your childhood, your life has probably been pretty steady and stable for the last few years. Sure, there have been ups and downs and you've changed and grown as a boy, but boyhood is usually marked by very slow and gradual development compared to the upcoming season in your life. But soon, instead of just hanging out at the end of the runway with the other fighter jets, instead of slowly taxiing back and forth on the runway, your life is about to accelerate in a very intense and rapid period called adolescence. And at the end of adolescence, you will take off into the sky for an even greater adventure: manhood.

Any fighter pilot will probably tell you that good preparation before the flight is essential to a successful mission. He has spent thousands of hours learning to fly. He has considered problems he could encounter and maneuvers he could use in those dangerous situations. He has tested and serviced the plane. He has filled it up with fuel. He has studied the specific flight plan, considered the weather, and learned the goal and details of the mission. The takeoff is but a few seconds; the mission is but a few hours; but the preparation is years in the making.

You are a man in the making. Before you race down that runway and head up into the sky, it's important and wise to make sure you are well prepared and equipped for the flight. You'd better make sure you know how to fly the plane and that it has fuel in it. You'd better know what you're going to do when you come under enemy attack. And, most importantly, you'd better know what the mission is and where you're going. It's easy to get lost in the vast sky without a plan.

Manhood is the same way. You'll be there before you know it, and if you haven't done your preparations in advance, you can make a lot of unnecessary mistakes as you're racing down the runway of adolescence. Not only will you make more mistakes without good preparation now, but you can cause yourself—and others—a lot of harm and heartache as well. You can crash on the runway or take off in the wrong direction, and you might never grow into the sort of man God designed you to be. We don't want you to crash or fly to the wrong destination or get lost in the sky.

This book is designed to give you a mission and flight plan:

- ♣ We'll tell you what your purpose is as a man. We'll tell you what it means to be a man: what your destination is.
- ♣ We'll tell you how to accelerate properly and safely down the short runway of adolescence you are about to begin.
- ♣ We'll tell you about some problems you are likely to encounter and how you can defeat them before they make you crash or change your flight plan.

✦ We'll encourage you to get some good co-pilots and flight instructors and technical staff, both your age and older men, who will support and help you on your journey.

So buckle up! The next few years of your life will be a great adventure. Changes like these are on the way:

✦ Your mind, body, emotions and relationships will be changing in ways that you can't fully understand until you have experienced them.

✦ You will feel new and more intense passions and desires.

✦ You will think about girls, your friends and your parents differently than you do now, and you will relate to them in new ways.

✦ You will think about yourself differently.

✦ You will long for more independence and new challenges.

✦ You will dream new dreams and develop your own identity.

Every adventure also has its share of difficulties and dangers. Self-esteem often dips during your teenage years (though many boys try to hide that on the outside). While you will enjoy and appreciate the increasing freedoms, they will bring temptations that can be hard to resist, and the consequences for a poor decision can be costly. While your body will grow in size and strength, it can be an awkward process with aches and acne. Girls can make your heart race and your heart break. All in all, adolescence can be like riding a roller coaster with many ups and downs.

In this book, we'll give you as complete and honest of a look at the journey ahead as we can. We want this to be authentic and cover the real issues and temptations that you will likely encounter in the upcoming months and years. We are addressing the topics that boys tell us are on their minds and that teenage boys say they are struggling with. While some of these topics can be embarrassing or difficult, we believe that it is better to know on the front end what you will probably face, and we want to help equip and prepare you for facing them.

But it's not just the next few years that we care about. We want you to have a vision for the sort of man God wants you to be when you have passed through the adolescent years. That's our ultimate goal. If you will set your eyes on the final goal—the sort of man you should become—then that will direct you in how you navigate the teenage years. Approaching challenges with the end result in mind is always the best way to begin. Great coaches begin the season talking about where they want the team to be at the end of the season. They talk about conference championships and bowl games and final rankings.

Coaches give their players a playbook to instruct them on how they want the game to be played. God has given you His playbook to help you navigate through the issues that you will be facing in the next few years. Boys are often surprised to hear that the Bible speaks on so many topics. Drinking, peer pressure, friendships, families, girls, even puberty and sex—the Bible gives us perspective and instruction in these matters. It speaks to the role and responsibilities of men. It tells you the sort of man, husband and father you should be one day. It tells all of us how to approach our work and worship and the girls and women in our lives. It talks about our self-worth, our successes, and the stuff we own, use and want to have. It covers difficulties and failures. It tells us about the forgiveness you can experience for all of our mistakes, including ones you may have already committed. We'll cover all of these topics in this book.

But even more than covering these topics, the Bible describes God's love for you. Rather than primarily advice and rules, the Bible, most importantly, is the true story of the good news of how much God loves us and how He is seeking to save us. It's the good news of what He has done for us rather than what we can do for Him. It's about what we can receive rather than what we must achieve.

We hope that by helping to develop your thinking about these teenage topics and understanding God's love, grace and pursuit of us, you will grow in wisdom and stature and favor with God and man. Our desire is that one day you will become a better man, husband and father, and we hope that you will, long before then, deepen your faith and walk with the Lord Jesus Christ; we hope you at least begin to explore questions in your mind and heart about who this God of the Bible is and what He means when He says in Jeremiah 29:11 that He has plans to grow and prosper you.

Chapter 1
Questions for Reflection and Discussion

1. What are some of the issues that you think will be difficult for you in the next few years?

2. Does the idea of becoming a man scare you or make you nervous? Why or why not?

3. If you could have one question answered about the road ahead for you, what would it be?

4. Is your dad available to talk with you about adolescence and the journey to manhood? If he is not available, who could you talk to about this important topic?

5. What do you hope to accomplish by reading and studying this book?

6. What is the best piece of advice your dad, mom, adult leader, coach, or mentor has given you so far?

7. How would you define manhood?

8. Do you view the upcoming years of your life as an adventure or just a regular part of your life? Why or why not?

Chapter 2

On Course Or Off Course?

He's a real nowhere man
Sitting in his nowhere land
Making all his nowhere plans
For nobody.
Doesn't have a point of view
Knows not where he's going to
Isn't he a bit like you and me?

— **John Lennon**, "Nowhere Man", Lead Singer of The Beatles

You see, my old man had a philosophy. Peace means having a bigger stick than the other guy.

— **Tony Stark**, From the Movie "Iron Man"

The tale of Flight 19 started on December 5th, 1945. Five Avenger torpedo bombers lifted into the air from the Naval Air Station in Fort Lauderdale, Florida, at 2:10 in the afternoon. It was a routine practice mission, and the flight was composed of all students except for the Commander, Lieutenant Charles Taylor.

The mission called for Taylor and his group of 13 men to fly due east 56 miles to Hens and Chicken Shoals to conduct practice bombing runs. When they had completed that objective, the flight plan called for them to fly an additional 67 miles east, and then turn north for 73 miles and finally straight back to base, for a total distance of 140 miles. This course would take them on a triangular path over the sea.

About 90 minutes after the flight had left, Lieutenant Robert Cox at the base picked up a radio transmission from Taylor. Taylor indicated that his compasses were not working, but he believed himself to be somewhere over the Florida Keys (the Keys are a long chain of islands south of the Florida mainland). Cox urged Taylor to fly north toward Miami if he was sure he was flying over the Keys.

Planes today have a number of ways that they can check their current position including listening to a set of GPS (Global Positioning Satellites) in orbit around the Earth. It is almost impossible for a pilot to get lost if he has the right equipment and uses it properly. In 1945, though, planes flying over water had to depend on knowing their starting point, how long and fast they had flown, and in what direction. If a pilot made a mistake with any of these figures, he was lost.

Apparently, Taylor had become confused at some point in the flight. He was an experienced pilot, but hadn't spent a lot of time flying east toward the Bahamas which was where he was headed on that day. For some reason Taylor thought the flight had started out in the wrong direction and had headed south toward the Keys, instead of east. This thought was to color his decisions throughout the rest of the flight with deadly results.

The more Taylor took his flight north to try to get out of the Keys, the further out to sea the Avengers actually traveled. As time went on, snatches of transmissions were picked up on the mainland indicating the other Flight 19 pilots were trying to get Taylor to change course. "If we would just fly west," one student told another, "we would get home." He was right.

By 4:45 P.M., it was obvious to the people on the ground that Taylor was hopelessly lost. He was urged to turn control of the flight over to one of his students, but he didn't. As it grew dark, communications deteriorated. From the few words that did get through, it was apparent Taylor was still flying north and east, the wrong direction.

At 5:50 P.M., the ComGulf Sea Frontier Evaluation Center managed to get a fix on Flight 19's weakening signal that was east of New Smyrna Beach, Florida. By then communications were so poor that this information could not be passed to the lost planes.

At 6:20 P.M., a Dumbo flying boat was dispatched to try and find Flight 19 and guide it back. Within the hour two more planes, Martin Mariners, joined the search. Hope was rapidly fading for Flight 19 by then. The weather was getting rough and the Avengers were very low on fuel.

The last transmission from Flight 19 was heard at 7:04 P.M. Planes searched the area through the night and the next day. There was no sign of the Avengers. Being off course and confused cost them their lives.

The journey to manhood can often be confusing. The landmarks that our culture provides for us often get us off course or even lost. One of the difficulties today for boys about to begin the journey to manhood is that no one has told them what it means to be a man. We've asked many twelve-year-olds what it means to be a man. We've also asked many teenage boys. We've asked men. We've asked dads and even moms. Not many people can even answer the question, let alone give a well-thought-out answer. Boys today are put in a difficult situation. They are being asked to begin the journey to manhood without a defined goal or a clear direction. Many boys today are being sent on a mission without a plan. They are being asked to work a puzzle with no idea about what they are trying to assemble. It's like hiking in unknown woods without a map or being the quarterback of a football team and not being told what the plays are. It's no wonder that many boys end up making poor choices during their teenage years.

The world we live in today tries to define manhood by what we see and hear. Television, the internet and music give us a very selfish view of the world. They teach lessons about manhood where you and only you are the most important person in the world. They urge you to do what feels good, do what makes you happy, do what is popular, do what makes you successful, and do what makes you cool. They do this by putting athletes, musicians and movie stars on a pedestal. Sadly, we see more negative examples than positive. Many people base their view of manhood by what these men do or don't do. This leads us to an inaccurate and unclear picture of manhood.

So, let's take some time to get a vision of the man God designed you to be. Let's look at the picture of a man that God paints. But first, we must focus on what it does not mean to be a man. We like to call them the myths of manhood. Myths are stories or ideas that aren't really true or accurate, even if many people believe them or are familiar with them. You've got to understand—and then dismiss—these myths of manhood before you can start to develop a vision of real manhood, sort of like becoming a good tennis player means you may have to unlearn the habit of hitting a backhand the wrong way before you can learn the proper backhand stroke.

So here are the lies or myths you shouldn't believe:

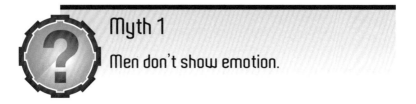

Myth 1
Men don't show emotion.

The first myth about manhood concerns our strength. As you grow into a man, your physical strength increases a lot. Your muscles will grow significantly during the teenage years. You'll probably look in the mirror as you flex your muscles, and you'll see health and sports magazines with pictures of men with bulging muscles. You will hope and dream of the day that you will have a "six pack." You will compare your body with the body of your friends and competitors. Teenage boys and men usually care a lot about their strength, or at least how strong other people think they are. However, because we tend to care so much about our strength, we sometimes think that as men we are weak if we show any emotion. Just because we are tough on the outside, we think that means we have to be tough on the inside also. Men hide their feelings because they do not want others to see them differently or make fun of them. Most men refuse to let anyone know they are hurting or afraid. They don't share their fears and emotions with friends, girlfriends and sometimes even their wives. Men often don't talk about relationships and, as they get older, they also struggle to discuss love. Our society makes men think only girls talk about that stuff. They do this often because they have bought into the myth that real men don't show emotion. Former Florida quarterback Tim Tebow shows us differently.

The 32-13 Alabama victory over Florida in the 2009 SEC Championship game was emotional for Gator Nation, but perhaps no one took it harder on the field than Tim Tebow, who was seen crying on the sidelines as the clock ticked down.

Tebow crying demonstrated the emotion he puts into the game, and it generated a variety of responses, both positive and negative. He continued to have tears when interviewed after the game. He is showing emotion. He is showing passion. He is showing how much he loves the game of football, the University of Florida, the fans, his teammates and his coaches.

This myth about men not showing emotion can get in the way of friendships—friendships you will need to live a fulfilling life. It's hard to develop true friendships—deep connections—when you don't share what's really on your heart and the important things running through your head. This type of friendship takes work, and that is why many men shy away from them. You need to work just as hard on friendships as you do with sports, grades and other activities that are important to you. A lack of true friendship leads to a lot of confusion, stress and anxiety.

Our need for strength can even get in the way of our relationship with God; we can think we don't need anyone, including God. We think we can get through the day just fine by ourselves. Too many men think of a spiritual life as something weak or as something women do. That is not God's intention for you.

Myth 2

Men should define themselves by their outward achievements and successes.

Our culture judges men by outward success and achievement. Often times, NFL quarterbacks are only judged by how many Super Bowls they have won. We look past a person's heart and make up our definition of success based on grades, wealth, popularity and athletic achievement. Dr. Tim Kimmel, author of *Raising Kids for True Greatness*, makes some great points about the difference between success and true greatness:

- ✦ Success looks inward; true greatness looks upward, then outward.
- ✦ Success is about my agenda; true greatness is about God's agenda.
- ✦ Success is about receiving; true greatness is about giving.
- ✦ Success worships what it sees in a mirror; true greatness grieves over what it sees through its windows.
- ✦ Success pays off for now; true greatness pays off forever.

I have learned that success is to be measured not so much by the positions that one has reached in his life as by the obstacles one has overcome while trying to succeed.

– Booker T. Washington, American Political Leader and Author

While we encourage you to set challenging goals and work hard, we caution you against letting your results dictate how you feel about yourself and how you define yourself. It's easy to make your trophies into idols. It's easy to become addicted to a cheering crowd when you score touchdowns; it's easy to become addicted to the praise of others who admire your artwork or your high grades. And if you're not achieving and succeeding as your classmates are, it's easy to get down on yourself. Don't confuse worldly success with significance. Your achievements won't give your life meaning, nor will a big house, the prestigious job or having the right stuff. God cares about the heart, but man looks at outward appearances (I Samuel 16:7). Get your significance from knowing God's love and care for you rather than relying on your abilities that will fade or comparisons that you cannot control.

Myth 3

Men should only pursue certain "cool" hobbies and interests.

Author Alvin Reid urges people to "find your passion and make it your ministry." We live in a culture that promotes certain passions over others. It is no surprise that sports is at the top of the list. Commercial spots for the Super Bowl are the most expensive and the most coveted. The problem is that in some people's eyes, certain activities are somehow more important or more masculine than other ones are. In many schools and parts of our country, various activities reign and play a key role in conferring male coolness or masculinity. There is nothing inherently better about athletics than art or acting. Who's to say if shooting a basketball is better than singing a solo? The important thing to remember is that God can use your passions for your good and for His glory. We should look at all hobbies and interests as a way for us to use our God-given abilities and talents to glorify Him and serve others.

As a rock star, I have two instincts. I want to have fun, and I want to change the world. I have a chance to do both.

– Bono, Lead Singer of U2

God tells us in Romans 12:6 and I Corinthians 12:4 and 28 that we all have different gifts and talents. He doesn't say which ones are more important. Sometimes, boys and men shy away from God-given passions and interests because of how we think other people will judge us. We may think that boys and men don't do those things. Sometimes, our friends and classmates make fun of certain hobbies. That's not right either. As a teenage boy and man, pursue passionately the things God has put on your heart. You will experience a richer, fuller life.

Real men do many different things, depending on their interests and gifts. They cook and play the piano. They read and write poetry. They draw and paint. They compose music and act in plays. They play chess and climb rocks. They enjoy cooperative activities as much or more than competitive ones. There are no right activities or hobbies for a man.

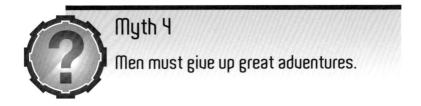

Myth 4
Men must give up great adventures.

Jack London, author of the book *White Fang*, when asked about purpose in life, responded by saying: "The proper function of man is to live, not to exist. I shall not waste my days in trying to prolong them. I shall use my time." At your age, you have incredible adventures ahead of you. As much as you love adventures, God loves them even more. We think He especially designed boys and men with adventuresome spirits. We men often love to explore, take risks and play and invent games in which we are challenged and pushed to the edge. This sense of adventure, however, can be misguided during the teenage years. Some adventures could lead down a path towards things like alcohol, drugs, vandalism and sex outside of marriage. These paths should be avoided. Your parents and schools will tell you that many things are out of bounds. When they give you these restrictions, it is important to honor and respect them, even if you feel like you are missing out on an adventure that other teenage boys are having.

This does not mean that there are no adventures left to enjoy. Your life is not meant to be boring and empty. Author Wilfred Peterson says, "A man practices the art of adventure when he breaks the chain of routine and renews his life through reading new books, traveling to new places, making new friends and taking up new hobbies." Men should never fall into the trap of believing that a life of adventure is over at a certain age. God called men of all ages and stages to a life of adventure. As you learn more about the character of God and His Son Jesus, you will come to see God as sending each of us on a great adventure when we become a follower of His. Jesus lived a radical and adventuresome life, and He calls us to live the same way. Real men embrace the right kinds of adventures.

Erik Weihenmayer has what some may call a disability, but he has not let that stop him from living a life of adventure. Weihenmayer feels at home climbing mountains. He's been climbing since his teenager years—right after a genetic disorder robbed him of his eyesight. Weihenmayer is blind. "I realized I would never run down the basketball court on a break away or, you know, catch a pop-fly, but I realized the adventure I wanted in my life wasn't dead. It was just starting," Weihenmayer said.

A graduate of Boston College, he has climbed many of the world's highest peaks. Two years ago, he set his sights on the world's highest mountain—Everest. He set off with a team of 21 climbers for an excursion that would take three months. He was the first blind climber to reach the summit of Mount Everest. His experience is detailed in a book and documentary.

"For kids who go blind, it's not a death sentence. I mean you have a great life ahead of you, of excitement, of adventure, or whatever your character allows you to do with your life," Weihenmayer said.

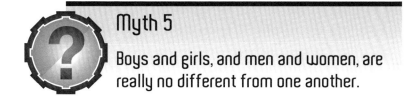

Myth 5

Boys and girls, and men and women, are really no different from one another.

God made you a boy! He is turning you into a man. Celebrate that. You are very different from your sister or that girl down the street. Boys and girls generally view and experience the world in different ways. Later in the book, we'll talk about girls. Part of why you will be so attracted to them is because they are different from you. Genesis tells us that God created women and men differently. You will one day learn that their key needs, the ways they prefer to communicate and to be loved, and the ways they interact with people, are probably different from you and your buddies. It's not better to be a boy or a girl, but it's different. Yes, both you and she were made in God's image, so you need to understand (and respect!) those differences.

Robert Lewis, in his book, *Raising a Modern Day Knight*, lists four responsibilities for godly men:

- ♣ Spiritual Leader
- ♣ Servant Leader

- ♣ Provider
- ♣ Protector

God assigns particular roles and responsibilities to men; He gives certain ones to women. Again, neither role is better or more important. As men, though, we'd better know what God expects from us, and we should start practicing it. Men in particular are passively sitting by and ignoring our unique responsibilities of taking the initiative and providing leadership and service. Too many men today are forgetting the sacrifices they are to make and the protection they are to provide—both for their communities and families. Know the type of leadership God expects of you and begin to look for men who model this well.

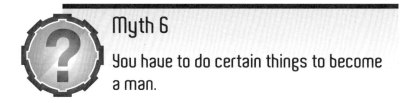

Myth 6
You have to do certain things to become a man.

In some societies around the world, it is very clear when a boy becomes a man. Usually, the boys and the men go away from their town or village on some sort of challenging adventure. They return together and have a ceremony in which everyone in the town or village attends. The purpose of this gathering is for everyone to know that the boys are now considered men. Sometimes, body piercings or marks serve to remind everyone of this new status.

In America today, though, there is no clear point at which a boy becomes a man. No one really knows. It's confusing to boys and adults. Boys usually want to be considered men (or at least no longer a child), so they have invented their own ceremonies and rites of passage into manhood because the men aren't doing this for them. The problem is, these rituals are almost always unhealthy, unwholesome and dangerous initiations. They usually involve things like drinking, smoking, using other drugs, fighting, having sex, joining a gang, shoplifting or engaging in some other dangerous activity to prove themselves. Of course, these things in no way make you a man.

Size and age also don't make you a man. Just because you grow bigger and stronger doesn't mean you are necessarily the real man God intends you to be. Every male becomes an adult, but not every adult male becomes, truly, a man. Growing into that man takes careful thought and planning. It takes discipline. It takes courage and endurance. It doesn't happen overnight, or when your body suddenly has the capabilities of an adult man, or when you enter a certain grade or turn a certain age or even get married. Becoming a real man is a life-long process, a journey and an incredible adventure. You must also remember that there are no shortcuts.

Every kid needs a mentor. Everybody needs a mentor.

– Donovan Bailey, Olympic Sprinter

You are about to go on the greatest journey of your life. You will need guides to keep you on the right path: mentors and parents and teachers and coaches who have already trekked where you are going and can tell you where the roads lead and where the dangers lie. There are forks in the road. You will have to make choices. There will be flashing neon signs telling you to get off the path. There will be friends who are waving you off the path or who are trekking down the wrong one. There will be apparent shortcuts and paths that look easy. Beware of such roads, even if a steady stream of cars seems to be headed that way. But if you will keep the map to manhood in front of you, if you will keep at the front of your mind where you are headed— knowing what it means to be a man—you are more likely to arrive there safely and in a way that is deeply rewarding. And that is our hope and prayer for you.

Chapter 2
Questions for Reflection and Discussion

1. When I am lonely, uncertain or afraid, do I have someone I talk to? If so, who is that person? If not, who do I wish I could talk to?

2. What two accomplishments am I most proud of? Am I too proud? If I were better at something, would I feel better about myself?

3. Is there something I really want to do or try, but I'm afraid of what other people will think?

4. What is the coolest adventure for a boy your age you've ever heard about?

5. Beside your body, how do you think you are different from a girl your age? How are your mom and dad different?

6. How do you become a man, and at what point does it happen?

7. Which myth of manhood are you most likely to believe?

8. What other myths of manhood do you think are out there?

9. Why do we believe certain myths of manhood?

Chapter 3

Flight Pattern

All that is necessary for the triumph of euil is that good men do nothing.

— **Edmund Burke,** British Statesman and Philosopher

Try not to become a man of success, but rather try to become a man of value.

— **Albert Einstein,** Physicist and Nobel Prize Winner

A route is a description of the path followed by an aircraft when flying between airports. Most commercial flights will travel from one airport to another, but private aircraft, commercial sightseeing tours, and military aircraft may often do a circular or out-and-back trip and land at the same airport from which they took off. The journey to manhood can often be seen the same way. Many boys follow the route they are supposed to and arrive at the destination successfully. There are boys who take a different route and end up landing at the same place they took off. Our goal in this chapter is to give you a route to follow. We want you to follow this flight pattern so that you will arrive at your destination of becoming a godly man.

So what does it mean to be a man? The answer to this question will be the focus of this chapter. We have looked at ways the world attempts to define manhood and exposed them as myths. Our definition of manhood centers around seven virtues we believe covers every area of a boy's life. We want to give you a definition that you can remember and apply to the issues you will face in the upcoming years. Our vision for real manhood is based on what God reveals to us about men.

Manhood– A real man glorifies God by seeking an adventuresome life of purpose and passion as he protects and serves others.

Real authentic manhood begins with purpose. Man's purpose in life is to glorify God in all he says and does. Do not let who you are or where you are from change your perspective. Your purpose is still the same: to glorify God in every situation. Real men also seek to live a life of adventure. Men are not called to live boring and dull lives. A life lived for the glory of God is anything but boring. It will take you on journeys that might make you uncomfortable or scared. It might push you to do things that the world might see as weird or different. One thing is for sure: a life lived for the glory of God is a life of adventure. Real men also live with passion. They are passionate about the things of God. Their hearts break for the things that break the heart of God. Real men use their passion and purpose to serve and protect others. Godly men seek to live a life of service to their family and community. Their passion to glorify God leads them to stand up for those who are in need. Godly men use God's Word as their guide. They seek to live by His standards and for His glory.

The Bible tells us about the character of God. It highlights examples of manly character and behavior that delights God, and it shows examples that disappoint Him. In Jesus Christ, the Bible tells us about the life of the only man ever to lead a perfect life. Jesus, as a man, faced many of the struggles and temptations that you as a teenager and man will encounter. He surrounded himself with friends, and he cared deeply about those friends. They presented him with some bad ideas; they disappointed and betrayed him. Jesus was tempted to use his power and popularity for his own comforts and convenience rather than serving others. He felt many of the emotions that you do: sadness, frustration, and disappointment, and joy, laughter and fulfillment. He knows first-hand the struggles and temptations you will face, but He also knows the sort of man you can become.

In the course of becoming a real man, you will grow to be more like Jesus, but because of the sinfulness of our world and even of our own flesh, we will never realize that perfection until Jesus comes again. As a result, we must prepare by practicing the virtues of manhood that are in alignment with God's righteous standards for us; we should strive to live them out. Over time, we should increasingly conform our lives to them. Our decisions and character should look more like Jesus every year. You should be more Christ-like at 16 than at 12, and more at 26 than at 16. Don't expect to be perfect. Know that you will mess up and must rely on God's grace to get you through this journey. It's awesome to know that we can claim Christ's perfect record for us.

So let's look specifically at the seven virtues of manhood that we believe will help you navigate the upcoming years. We believe this will give you a clear vision for manhood and will give you a set of glasses to help you look at the world in a different way. Read carefully and pay close attention! This chapter will be the foundation for the rest of the book. The seven virtues that we define and describe will serve as a guide in your journey to true and authentic manhood.

VIRTUE 1

Virtue 1

The True Friend: Leave No Man Behind

When you think about your friends, you probably think about people you enjoy spending time with. You probably have something in common with them. You're on the same sports team, or you have math class together, or you have similar interests. Maybe you're friends because you live in the same neighborhood or because your parents are friends with their parents. You probably consider someone your friend because he is nice to you most of the time, or maybe he makes you laugh.

A true friendship, though, is much deeper than just having common interests and experiences. Godly men are willing to stick with their friends through thick and thin. True friends endure tough times. They make the commitment to leave no man behind.

True friends:

- ♣ Develop such trust with one another that they can share anything—and everything—that is happening in their lives.
- ♣ Talk about their feelings, their frustrations, and their failures.
- ♣ Share openly and honestly with one another.
- ♣ Encourage and serve one another.
- ♣ Stand up for each other.

✦ True friends can also say difficult things to each other. If one man is making poor choices, a true friend will lovingly tell him and help redirect him. True friends hold one another accountable; they don't look the other way when one could be headed for trouble.

A friend loves at all times, and a brother is born for adversity.

– Proverbs 17:17

In today's world, most men are looking for friends that only benefit them. True friendship takes work and requires you to be selfless. Men need friends who love, help and support them.

You might be surprised to learn that many men—maybe most men—don't have a single true friend. They may have golfing buddies or some guys they hunt with, but they don't necessarily have anyone with whom they share what's really on their heart. Their friendships are superficial; they aren't emotional, heart-to-heart friendships. Too many men are afraid to talk about their struggles, about the loneliness and emptiness and questions that often reside deep in their hearts. They think it will make them seem weak, and as we discussed in the last chapter, men feel a need to project strength.

Friendship is the hardest thing in the world to explain. It's not something you can be taught in school; and if you haven't learned the value of friendship, You haven't really learned anything at all.

– Muhammed Ali, Boxer

Most men think they don't need to share their true feelings with anyone else. Men keep themselves busy with work and activities so they do not have to engage in real conversations. This leads some men to go through life without ever developing true friendships. A life without true friendship often leads to loneliness and isolation. Real men surround themselves with friends who are willing to stick with them through thick and thin.

Consider this story about two friends who were walking through the desert. In a specific point of the journey, they had an argument, and one friend slapped the other one in the face.

The one who got slapped was hurt, but without anything to say, he wrote in the sand, "TODAY, MY BEST FRIEND SLAPPED ME IN THE FACE."

They kept on walking until they found an oasis where they decided to take a swim. The one who got slapped and hurt started drowning, and the other friend saved him. When he recovered from the fright, he wrote on a stone, "TODAY MY BEST FRIEND SAVED MY LIFE."

The friend who saved and slapped his best friend asked him, "Why, after I hurt you, did you write in the sand, and now you write on a stone?"

The other friend, smiling, replied, "When a friend hurts us, we should write it down in the sand, where the winds of forgiveness get in charge of erasing it away, and when something great happens, we should engrave it in the stone of the memory of the heart, where no wind can erase it."

Real men are secure and strong enough to share their emotions and vulnerabilities, and they are smart enough to know that having a true friend will make their lives more rewarding and fulfilling. They also know that God calls us to serve and love others, to look at their hearts, and to share and speak honestly with one another—all hallmarks of being a true friend.

We hope you will understand the real basis of genuine friendships and that you will begin working on the skills of becoming a true friend. It will help you to make wiser decisions in the upcoming years. True friends will give you the support you need during the difficult days of being a teenager and they will make your life much more meaningful as a man. True friendships don't come naturally to a lot of men, but they can be one of life's greatest blessings to the man who is able to develop them.

VIRTUE 2

Virtue 2

The Humble Hero: Develop A God Sized Vision

We live today in a world with many celebrities but very few heroes. If you are like most boys, you will probably have a hard time coming up with a hero other than a sports figure, movie star or musician. Being famous, though, doesn't make someone a hero. In fact, being famous usually makes people more prideful and selfish, and we already live in a very selfish world.

A hero is someone who has a big and noble purpose for his life. He develops a God sized vision. Julie Ferweda, author of *One Million Arrows*, says "Anyone can receive a promise or vision and get busy working towards it on his own, but without the continuous guidance of the Holy Spirit, grand plans taken into our own hands fall flat, or worse, lead us into trouble. It's the faithful years of relationship with God, one prayer at a time, where great, world changing work is accomplished."

Humble Heroes have a plan:

- ✦ His plan isn't about himself; it's about the world.
- ✦ His plan isn't about winning a game, but it's about improving the world in a way that flows from the passions God put on his heart and the gifts he has been given.
- ✦ He seeks God's will for his life, not the pursuit of things that will bring him comfort, prosperity and fame.
- ✦ His reward is not a cheering crowd or a big bank account. He finds his reward in the Lord.

True heroes are not necessarily well known, and they are not always successful in the way the world defines success. Heroes don't have to be CEO's of a company or on TV or written up in history books, but they lead significant lives, and they lead lives of service. They have a focus. They have a purpose: a purpose for which they will sacrifice, even for which they will lay down their life.

In the spring of 2004, Austin Gutwein watched a video that showed children who had lost their parents to AIDS. After watching the video, he realized these kids weren't any different from him except they were suffering. Austin felt God calling him to do something to help them. He decided to shoot free throws and on World AIDS Day, 2004, he shot 2,057 free throws to represent the 2,057 kids who would be orphaned during his day at school. Friends and family sponsored Austin, and he was able to raise almost $3,000. That year, the money was used by World Vision to provide hope to eight orphan children.

From that year forward, thousands of people have joined Austin in a basketball shoot-a-thon called *Hoops of Hope*. By doing something as simple as shooting free throws, *Hoops of Hope* participants have raised over $1 million. The children left behind by AIDS now have access to food, clothing, shelter, a new school and, finally, a medical testing facility which he was told would save an entire generation. A second clinic is now under construction.

Austin believes that anyone, no matter what their age or skills, can make a difference. Austin has developed a God sized vision for his life.

While we encourage you to develop a heroic purpose for your life, we just as strongly encourage you to pursue it with a humble spirit. Humility is the opposite of arrogance. It is so tempting to think we are responsible for all of the blessings, successes and significance in our lives. We can think that our hard work and talent is all we need and makes all the difference. If you don't maintain a humble spirit, your arrogance will go against the heroic purpose you are pursuing. It will turn people off, and you will lose your effectiveness. Men, in particular, struggle with success. Be careful to be humble. Proverbs 3:34 tells us that God mocks the proud but gives grace to the humble.

Just as there are many men without true friends, there also are millions of men today without any heroic purpose for their lives. Though many men appear successful and powerful, they are leading lives of "quiet desperation," as author Henry David Thoreau said. They are bored and restless and empty. Their lives have little meaning to them. For many of them, they thought that the purpose of life was simply to earn good grades, be successful, get the right job, marry a nice girl, live in a big house and generally be a good person. All those things indeed are good, but if that's all there is to a man's life, he will one day realize that his life lacks a heroic purpose, and this leads to despair. The sooner you understand that you need a heroic purpose for your life, the sooner you will experience the fullness of life.

Virtue 3

The Servant Leader: I Am Third

Boys and men crave leadership positions. We want to be the captain of the team, sing the solo in the musical, and be elected to the student government. We aspire to lead the company, the city, and the church. We want to lead because we believe it will make us successful. We are all sinners, and selfishness is certainly a part of the sinfulness we all have. In many ways, we want to be leaders for selfish reasons: we get privileges and perks as leaders. They become popular. They usually make more money. They are given power, and power feels good.

Servant leadership, though, centers on using the position, power and prestige of leadership to serve other people. A servant leader recognizes that his relationship with Christ is first, his relationship with others is second, and that he is third. Jesus displayed this so beautifully when He served His disciples by washing their dirty feet. What an incredible example for the God of the universe, with all of His power, to get down on his knees to meet a common need of someone else.

Alex and Brett Harris' book, *Do Hard Things*, details the story of twelve-year old Zach Hunter, a true servant leader.

When he was twelve years old, Zach Hunter was confronted with a painful fact: 27 million people around the world still live in slavery, and half of them are children. Zach's shocking encounter with that reality grew into a campaign against modern day slavery that has taken this soft spoken teen from the Atlanta suburbs to the main stages of the nation's largest Christian music festivals and far beyond.

Zach launched *Loose Change to Loosen Chains (LC2LC)*, a campaign to raise money and awareness for the fight against modern-day slavery. The concept was simple: encourage his peers to gather and give their loose change, which then went to deserving organizations working to free slaves around the world. Zach raised almost ten thousand dollars in the initial drive. Zach's plan has transformed him from a kid who suffers anxiety attacks to a sixteen-year-old who has spoken to more than half a million people at live events, has appeared on national television numerous times, has written two books, and even delivered a speech at the White House.

> We can make a difference in the lives of slaves. It doesn't really matter how young we are. It doesn't matter if we have physical, mental, or emotional disabilities. It doesn't matter the color of our skin or where we're from. Anybody can make a difference and be a voice for the voiceless.
>
> – Zach Hunter, 16

Real men are servant leaders. They serve others, even when it is unpopular. Their leadership is more courageous than comfortable. It gives power to the powerless. It displays a passion for those Scripture describes as the "least, lost and the lonely."

Servant leadership is not easy because it is not natural. It is opposite to our sinful nature. It's not what the world celebrates. As a man, you will feel the pressure of competition and the need to get ahead at all costs, and that the only way to get ahead is to leave others behind. You will sometimes sense that service is not manly. You will see all around you that success almost always seems manly but that servant-hood usually is not.

Be courageous in your leadership. As you embrace this concept, you will increasingly find yourself able to confidently make decisions that are different from what many teenagers do. You will stand firm in a sometimes-uncertain world, and you will stand out as a real man.

Virtue 4

The Moral Motivator: Make a Difference

God expects certain things from our schools and communities. His standards are high. He wants them to be characterized by love and compassion. He wants us to treat each other fairly, and with respect and equality, regardless of a person's race, ethnicity or background. He cares deeply about the poor telling us numerous times in the Bible to look after them. God wants our society to be fair and just and based on deep principles—His instructions. After all, we are His children and created in His image, so it is not surprising that He wants us to build communities in which everyone is respected, loved and treated fairly. A Moral Motivator makes a difference in his community by using his God-given gifts and talents to serve those who are in need.

You do not have to wait until you are older to make a difference. There are ways you can serve your community right now. The organization *Kids Can Make a Difference* lists ways that students are making a difference in their communities:

1 Two sixth grade students in Concord, New Hampshire wrote to all 100 U.S. Senators about a bill the Senate was discussing dealing with the homeless. They had done their "homework" and presented their arguments in a highly professional manner. They received responses from nearly every Senator (or a member of his/her staff) explaining the Senator's position.

2 Seventh grade students in South Portland, Maine conducted a program at the Portland Museum of Art entitled "Celebrating The Arts In Honor of World Hunger Education." This same class "adopted" a single parent family living in a local shelter and provided them "with a Christmas they will never forget."

3 A Chicago community health clinic that provides services for poor, pregnant women and infants was about to be shut down for lack of funds. Fifty children organized a protest in front of the clinic drawing the attention of the media and lawmakers. The clinic remained open.

4 Fourth Grade students in Kittery Maine ran a canned food drive at their school and donated the food to the local food pantry. Representatives of the classes helped prepare the food for distribution to the clients of the food pantry.

5 Students from the sixth grade at a private school in New York City gave up a weekend to help raise funds for World Hunger Year. Some of them were on the phone bank during the annual HUNGERTHON radio show.

6 A seventh grade student researched the topic of hunger for an honors program he was taking at his school in New Jersey. He developed a theory for ending world-wide hunger and presented the results of his findings to the World Hunger Year Board of Directors.

7 First through sixth grade students at Presbyterian Day School in Memphis give up their snacks one day each month and donate them to the Ronald McDonald House for families with children who have been diagnosed with cancer.

When men don't care about the impact of their plans and decisions on others, it is easy for members of a community to be exploited, taken advantage of, and disregarded. For all of the wonderful things about our great country, we have large segments of our population who are poor, who don't enjoy the same opportunities and social and economic justice that many others do. As business leaders or community leaders, you will find yourselves with opportunities to create policies or plans in your own best interest. Will you think about the rest of your community as you make such decisions? Will you look after the needs of the poor? Will you serve them?

Real men recognize that the only consideration to be taken into account in making plans is not how it affects them. They don't overlook others. They certainly don't bully other people or pick on others. They think about other people. Real men are motivated to build communities that are moral. Injustices offend them. The poor and under-resourced grieve their hearts. They have a strong desire to fix these things. They are moral motivators. As a teenager, you can shape the teenage world around you. Care about what you give to your school, friends and your community, not just what they give to you. If you develop now a heart for your school and the community around you, as a man you will be much more likely to care about the city in which you live and how you can serve it. Make a difference now!

Virtue 5

The Bold Adventurer: Don't Sit Around

Different authors have written that the story of man is God calling him out from where he is (often a place that is comfortable), taking him on an unknown and exciting adventure, and giving him a new name. God does this to Abram who becomes Abraham, Jacob who becomes Israel, Simon who becomes Peter, and Saul who becomes Paul. God sent them to new lands. He wrestled with them. He blinded them. Men of the Bible ventured into the wilderness and to the tops of mountains. They encountered storms and high seas, lions and lepers. They didn't lead boring lives and sit around all day with their equivalent of the sofa and remote control. No, they dreamed and dared. They took risks and chances. They had a wild and adventuresome spirit. They allowed God to take them where He wanted, to use them how He wanted. They gave their lives over to God. Being a bold adventurer does not mean that you just drop everything and go live a life in the wilderness just for the sake of being adventuresome. Bold adventurers live with a purpose greater than themselves.

Greg Mortenson is the co-founder of nonprofit Central Asia Institute, founder of Pennies For Peace, and co-author of the #1 New York Times bestseller *Three Cups of Tea*, and author of *Stones into Schools*. In July 1992, Mortenson's sister, Christa, died from a massive seizure after a lifelong struggle with epilepsy. The following year to honor his sister's memory, Mortenson climbed Pakistan's K2, the world's second highest mountain in the Karakoram range.

While recovering from the climb in a village called Korphe, Mortenson met a group of children sitting in the dirt writing with sticks in the sand and he made a promise to help them build a school.

From that rash promise grew a remarkable humanitarian campaign, in which Mortenson has dedicated his life to promote education, especially for girls, in remote regions of Pakistan and Afghanistan.

As of 2009, Mortenson has established or significantly supports 131 schools in rural and often volatile regions of Pakistan and Afghanistan, which provide education to over 58,000 children, including 44,000 girls; these children had few education opportunities before this campaign.

Mortenson is a living hero to rural communities of Afghanistan and Pakistan, where he has gained the trust of Islamic leaders, military commanders, government officials and tribal chiefs from his tireless effort to champion education, especially for girls.

He is one of few foreigners who has worked extensively for sixteen years (over 72 months in the field) in rural villages where few foreigners go.

TV newscaster Tom Brokaw calls Mortenson "one ordinary person, with the right combination of character and determination, who is really changing the world."

Most men gave up on adventures a long time ago. They have settled for boredom and comfort over adventure and purpose. They think that adventures are only for teenagers or young men. They wrongly believe that they have outgrown adventures, so they work and watch TV, collect their paychecks, and grow bored and depressed. Other men, because they have no sense of adventure, pursue fake and shallow things they think might give them an adventure. They leave their wives for an affair or girlfriend; they suddenly buy fancy clothes and cars; they medicate themselves with alcohol and drugs.

Growing into a man is a great adventure. Being a man with a heroic purpose is a great adventure. Living by God's standards, rather than the world's, is a great adventure. Serving others is a great adventure. God put an adventuresome spirit in your heart.

Don't sit around and let that spirit sit idle and waste away.

VIRTUE 6

Virtue 6

The Noble Knight: Called to Duty

When you think about a knight, a vision of a man in armor, battling another man, probably comes to mind. While knights were known for the battles they fought, they did so not out of a love of blood and fighting, but out of a sense of duty. They knew that, as men, they were given the responsibility to provide, protect and defend their families, friends and communities. They were courageous in how they sought to serve others. They were willing to put their lives on the line for their beliefs.

Noble knights lived by a code of honor and integrity. Principles, not conveniences and comforts, motivated them. They placed a high value on chivalry and civility, because they understood that displaying excellent manners was a way to show and provide respect to their friends, families and communities. Families were stronger and communities were safer because of the noble knights who took the lead in promoting and strengthening them.

World War II produced many heroes. One such man was Butch O'Hare. He was a fighter pilot assigned to an aircraft carrier in the South Pacific.

One day his entire squadron was sent on a mission. After he was airborne, he looked at his fuel gauge and realized that someone had forgotten to top off his fuel tank. He would not have enough fuel to complete his mission and get back to his ship. His flight leader told him to return to the carrier.

Reluctantly, he dropped out of formation and headed back to the fleet. As he was returning to the mothership, he saw something that turned his blood cold. A squadron of Japanese Zeroes were speeding their way toward the American fleet. The American fighters were gone on a sortie, and the fleet was all but defenseless. He couldn't reach his squadron and bring them back in time to save the fleet, nor could he warn the fleet of the approaching danger.

There was only one thing to do. He must somehow divert them from the fleet. Laying aside all thoughts of personal safety, he dove into the formation of Japanese planes. Wing-mounted 50 calibers were blazing as he charged in, attacking one surprised enemy plane and then another. Butch weaved in and out of the now broken formation and fired at as many planes as possible until finally all his ammunition was spent.

Undaunted, he continued the assault. He dove at the Zeroes, trying to at least clip off a wing or tail, in hopes of damaging as many enemy planes as possible and rendering them unfit to fly. He was desperate to do anything he could to keep them from reaching the American ships. Finally, the exasperated Japanese squadron took off in another direction.

Deeply relieved, Butch O'Hare and his tattered fighter limped back to the carrier. Upon arrival he reported in and related the event surrounding his return. The film from the camera mounted on his plane told the tale. It showed the extent of Butch's daring attempt to protect his fleet. He was recognized as a hero and given one of the nation's highest military honors.

Today, O'Hare Airport in Chicago is named in tribute to the courage of this great man.

Today, many men shrink from the responsibilities and duties needed of them. They don't take the initiative in strengthening their families. They aren't the spiritual leaders of the family, as God tells them to be. They run from conflicts. They make excuses. They run out on families. Many men honor their commitments and word only as long as they are convenient and comfortable and make them happy. The world today doesn't always seem to give much value to honor. Cheating seems OK as long as we don't get caught and as long as the pay-off is great. Many men say that manners are outdated. We often don't treat our peers and elders with much respect.

Real men, though, are noble knights. They have a code of principles they are going to live by, no matter what. They have integrity—they are the same person no matter what the circumstances; they do the right thing when no one is looking. They are going to take the initiative in providing for others and in protecting and defending their friends, families and communities. They step up to the plate to face difficult situations. They take responsibility for their actions. They are respectful, honest and well mannered. And they are courageous. You are called to duty. Go get in the action!

VIRTUE 7

Virtue 7

The Heart Patient: Give Up Control

Have you ever seen a doctor perform open-heart surgery? The heart patient is powerless. He lies unconscious on the operating table. He has put his trust—his whole life, in fact—in the hands of the doctors. The patient has surrendered his power and control to the doctor, and he hopes to awake with a better heart: one without disease and weaknesses.

We are all born with hearts that, spiritually, are diseased and dying—hearts in need of surgery. They are full of unwholesome desires, selfish wishes, jealousies, pride, anger, guilt and brokenness.

Paul's words in Romans 7:18-24 model this kind of reflection for us. "I realize that I don't have what it takes. I can will it, but I can't do it. I decide to do good, but I don't really do it; I decide not to do bad, but then I do it anyway. My decisions, such as they are, don't result in actions. Something has gone wrong deep within me and gets the better of me every time. It happens so regularly that it's predictable. The moment I decide to do good, sin is there to trip me up. I truly delight in God's commands, but it's pretty obvious that not all of me joins in that delight. Parts of me covertly rebel, and just when I least expect it, they take charge. I've tried everything and nothing helps. I'm at the end of my rope. Is there no one who can do anything for me? Isn't that the real question?" (The Message)

That's the bad news. The good news is that God promises to give us a new heart. We just have to ask Him.

Create in me a clean heart, O God, and renew a right spirit within me.

– Psalm 51:10

We have to come to the hospital, check ourselves in, and get on the operating table for God to do His work in our lives. It's an incredible gift: one that we can't earn and don't deserve. It's called grace. Grace is a gift of God that we do not deserve and cannot earn.

At 19 years old, Bruce Olson did something many of us wouldn't dare do. Only a Christian of five years, he sensed God calling him to the Amazon Indians of South America. With a few dollars in his pocket and no ability to speak Spanish, he hopped on a plane to Venezuela, unsure of what to expect. In 1962, Bruce made contact with the Motilone Indians—the first outsider to do so and survive.

The Motilone, a stone-age Indian tribe living in the rain forest on the border of Venezuela and Colombia, almost killed Bruce. They shot him with an arrow through his thigh but allowed him to live. Over the next few years, he slowly and painstakingly learned their language and became one of them. In time, he heard them recount a legend of a blond haired prophet who would bring "banana stalks" containing knowledge of life and God.

As the Indians learned about Jesus, God's Spirit transformed the previously violent tribe to such an extent that a visiting anthropologist, Samuel Greenberg, noticed. It triggered his own spiritual journey and some years later he became a Christian. The book *Bruchko and the Motilone Miracle* goes on to describe the profound advancements the Motilone made after their spiritual awakening.

God performed heart surgery on the people of this tribe. The result was a transformed group of heart patients.

Faith is a living and unshakable confidence, a belief in the grace of God so assured that a man would die a thousand deaths for its sake

– Martin Luther, German Theologian and Scholar

God's grace is powerful and liberating; it cleanses us from all of the baggage and junk we carry in our hearts in a fallen world. By accepting Jesus Christ as your personal Lord and Savior, God attributes to you a perfect heart because of what Jesus did on the cross. The sooner you understand this, and we mean really internalize this, the sooner you can lead joyful lives—not perfect lives, but joyful lives, knowing that all your sins, including the ones you will commit as a teenager and as a man, have been forgiven. The joy from knowing this should make you want to live your life in a way that is pleasing to God.

Heart patients must be willing to give up control of their lives in order to live for Christ. This might be uncomfortable, as heart surgery is a painful process. It requires change. You must spend time rehabilitating. There will be times when you are exhausted. It is worth it. God will transform you for your good and for His glory!

Manhood– A real man glorifies God by seeking an adventuresome life of purpose and passion as he protects and serves others.

The vision has been set before you:

 Leave No Man Behind

 Develop A God-Sized Vision

 You Are Third

 Make A Difference

 Don't Sit Around

 Called To Duty

 Give Up Control

Godly men develop true friendships by leaving no man behind. They understand their purpose and develop a God-sized vision for their life. They serve others by giving up control of their lives to God and realizing they are third. Real men use their passion to glorify God and make a difference in their community. Godly men are called to duty. They seek to serve and protect others. Real men don't sit around but lead adventuresome lives. They allow God to use them where He wants and how He wants.

We hope this Godly vision of what it means to be a man will inspire your journey to manhood. We hope it assures you, encourages you, and gives you hope. Now that you know what it means to be a man, let's see how you can live that out as you encounter the exciting yet dangerous challenges, opportunities and temptations of the years to come, starting with friends and peer pressure.

Chapter 3
Questions for Reflection and Discussion

1. Who is the best example of a great man? Why did you pick him?

2. Are you strong enough to share your weaknesses—and the things on your heart—with your friends? What is on your heart right now that is burdening you?

3. Who is a hero to you? What makes him a hero?

4. What is the difference between a celebrity and a hero?

5. How can you be a servant leader at school, home and in your community during the next month?

6. At your school or in your community, what seems immoral to you? What can you do about it?

7. What would be a really adventuresome thing for you to do? What is a really adventuresome thing for a middle school boy to do? What is a really adventuresome thing for a high school boy to do? What about for a dad?

8. Who do you know that really needs protection this week? What can you do to provide that protection?

9. Have you started thinking about a mission statement for your life?

10. Have you asked God for a new heart? Why or why not?

Chapter 4

Who Is Going To Be Your Wing Man?

None of us should wander alone, you least of all.

— *Lord of the Rings*

If you have two friends in your lifetime, you're lucky.
If you have one good friend, you're more than lucky.

— Bryon Douglas, *That Was Then, This Is Now*, by S.E. Hinton

It was 1952. Fighter pilot Robinson Risner flew his F-86 over North Korea with his wingman Lt. Joe Logan alongside him.

Already a jet ace—an elite title meaning he had shot down five enemy aircraft—Risner was escorting bombers in an attack on a chemical plant when the fuel tank of Logan's plane was hit.

Instead of letting Logan crash in enemy territory, Risner attempted a dangerous move. He nosed his plane into the back of Logan's and pushed him 60 miles through heavy enemy flak to an Air Force detachment where he could bail out safely. It was a heroic effort.

In your life, you will need friends who are willing to push you along when you cannot make it yourself. True friends "leave no man behind" even if it means taking a risk. The upcoming years will be difficult, and you will need solid friendships to help you get through them.

Who are my friends? Why are they my friends? What do my friends really think about me? What friend should I invite to spend the night? Will my closest friends be in my class? It's somewhat natural to spend a lot of time thinking about friends and friendships, because you spend more time with them most days than you do with your family. To some extent you are, for the first time, starting to build a life outside of your parents. And it is your friends who are, to some degree, replacing them.

Friends are important at every stage of life, but especially around the teenage years, and it is probably during these years that you will first realize just how crucial they are. You will realize that they can be important to your well-being and sense of identity. Let's look for a minute at the benefits of having friends. Some of those benefits include the following:

- They provide companionship and keep you from being lonely.
- They make you laugh.
- They give you the confidence to try new things and grow.
- They validate you, helping you to believe you are good and important.
- They teach you relationship skills.
- They offer support.
- They provide stability in a changing world and in a time in your life of great changes.

There are advantages to having friends, but it's not easy to develop meaningful and lasting friendships. Most guys your age do not understand what it means to be a true friend. This causes you to try and figure it out on your own. In most cases, we base our friendships on what the world values as opposed to what God values.

As important as friends are, know that it's OK if you don't yet have a true friend as we will define it in this chapter. It takes a lot of maturity, as well as time, on the part of two people to have a deep and meaningful friendship. The main thing is to be striving for developing the right type of friendships and then be patient. Know that a true friend can come from various places, including from your own family. And know there's not a right number of friends to have. As with so many other things, the quality of friendships is more important than their quantity.

But how do you know? For each person, deciding who true friends are is a difficult decision. It might be of benefit for you to develop some sort of personal grouping system of your friends. Depending on what group they fall into will determine how strong an influence you allow them to have in your life.

One possible classification scheme might be as follows:

1. Not Your Friend: People you usually don't associate with under normal circumstances.

2. Acquaintance: This group of people includes those that you might see in school, but you don't associate with out of school. You might occasionally cross their path out of school, but you wouldn't normally seek them out.

3. Wannabe Friends: These are people you might want to be friends with for some selfish reasons, such as hoping to be more popular. People who fall into this category are never your true friends because the foundation for the friendship does not have a solid basis.

4. True Friends: These are the ones in the small, close group of people that you confide in and you know that they have your best interest in mind. The people in this group are those whose influence on your life makes you a better person.

The Bible gives us a great example of true friendship. Jonathan and David were two guys close to your age that developed a true friendship based on things much deeper and more significant than similar interests and backgrounds.

If you've studied the Bible, you know that after David, a teenager, kills the Philistine giant Goliath, he develops a true friendship with Jonathan, the son of King Saul, whose people had been intimidated and threatened for years by the Philistines.

The first thing to note about their relationship is their very different backgrounds. Jonathan is the son of the king. He is a prince. He is a teenager of privilege, prestige, power and money. He grew up in a palace. He is supposed to be the king one day. David's background is very different. He is a shepherd from a very ordinary family of modest means. He was probably poor, in fact. David and Jonathan seem to have nothing in common. If they were alive today, they wouldn't go to the same school, live in the same neighborhood, play on the same teams, or have the same toys, or go on trips together. They probably wouldn't even know each other. Their friendship—probably the best example of true friendship in the Bible except for the friendship Jesus displays—teaches us that having the same background or interests isn't the basis for a true friendship.

David was Jonathan's biggest threat to becoming king. Instead of finding a way to get rid of him, Jonathan did something unbelievable. He took off his armor and then gave David his bow and his sword. Jonathan gave David weapons that could be used against him. What a selfless act. This is a great picture of what it means to be in a true friendship. True friends are willing to give up their needs, wants and desires for the sake of the friendship. Jonathan's unselfish act led David to have many trusted friends, many of which had more military accomplishments than he did. David surrounded himself with men that he trusted. Together, David and his friends were able to accomplish more than any one man could accomplish alone.

Don't judge a person and his potential for being a true friend, on whether or not he is similar to you. You should be friends with people from different backgrounds and races with different interests and resources.

Since their backgrounds couldn't serve as the basis for their friendship, they built it on something else—other things that are far more important. They built their friendship on their trust, common beliefs and serving each other. These are characteristics of true friendship.

So what does it mean to be a true friend? Here are some characteristics that we feel true friends must have:

1 True friends sacrifice. David and Jonathan sacrificed for one another. Would you give up your part in the school play or student government for a friend? Would you give a friend something that costs you dearly?

2 True friends tell each other about whatever is on their hearts. They share fears and hopes. They talk about God. They comfort each other. They don't just send text messages and talk on Facebook. They talk about the meaningful things. If something really hard is going on in your life (like your parents are getting divorced), do you have a friend that you can share that with? Are you willing to listen to your friend if they are having trouble?

3 True friends say difficult things to each other. Jonathan tells David difficult things about his family and that his father is planning to kill David. They speak the truth in a loving way. Can you tell your friends the truth about things even if it's not pleasant, or even if it will get you in trouble? Can you tell your friend that he is doing something wrong, when he is hurting himself or others? Can you really say what is on your heart?

4 True friends display unfailing kindness. Jonathan says, "Show me unfailing kindness" (I Samuel 20:14). That's not kindness when it's convenient or when it's easy. That's not ever partial kindness. When was the last time you did something truly kind for a friend? We don't mean calling up a friend to see if he wants to come over to play chess or spend the night. We mean doing something that does not benefit you.

5 True friends are loyal. They stick with each other no matter the circumstance. Both David and Jonathan loved the Lord and sought to follow his commandments. Their loyalty to God bound them to one another. Are you willing to give up an activity that you want to do in order to be there for your friend? When someone talks badly about your friends, do you stick up for them, or do you just let it go?

6 True friends serve each other. At the Last Supper, Jesus got down on his knees and washed the feet of his closest friends, the disciples. He then asked his disciples in John 13:12, "Do you understand what I have done for you? You call me teacher and Lord, and rightly so, for that is what I am. Now that I, your Lord and teacher, have washed your feet, you should also wash one another's feet. Now that you know these things, you will be blessed if you do them." Are you willing to serve your friends even if it means sacrificing your reputation?

As you reflect on the friendship that God gives us as a model, we hope you realize it's not based on doing things together; it's not based on having the same interest as someone else; it's not based on popularity; it's not something that changes; in short, it's quite different than most friendships you will have during the teenage years.

We have given you a Biblical example in David and Jonathan but we also want to give you a modern day example of someone who has gone through the journey ahead and made it out successfully because of friendships he established when he was your age. Hank was a seventh grader when God put on his heart to develop some meaningful friendships. Hank knew that the next few years were going to be full of challenges. He knew that it would be difficult to navigate through these alone. Hank made a decision to surround himself with a group of friends that would walk with him and support him during his middle and high school years. He chose friends that would be committed to making good decisions when faced with alcohol, drugs and how to treat women. Hank and his friends were so committed to each other that they created and signed a modern day covenant that said they would not drink or do drugs. Hank has recently graduated from high school and kept the covenant. This a powerful example of true friends taking a stand together and holding each other accountable for their actions. We hope this story encourages you to develop some true friendships to help you on your journey.

There are a lot of very shallow friendships during the teenage years—friendships that disappoint and hurt you, friendships that come and go, and friendships that can lead you astray. Don't confuse popularity with friendship. Being popular or cool doesn't mean you are a true friend and doesn't mean you are immune to the hurts of friendships. If you want to be a friend with someone so you will appear cooler and fit in, you are not being a true friend. If all you do is aspire to be popular, all you will have are shallow friends and short-lived friendships because you and your "friends" are being shallow and selfish and not serving each other. Be more than a shallow friend.

In the movie *October Sky*, we see the story of friends who committed themselves to each other even though they were not the most "popular" guys. Inspired by the launch of the Soviet Union's rocket Sputnik (October, 1957), a high school student in West Virginia named Homer Hickam decides to make his own rockets. Despite his father's initial opposition, Homer and his "outsider" friends persist and succeed. Homer and his friends were made fun of and picked on by other classmates. Against all odds, the boys win the national science fair with an entry describing their rockets. All of the boys go to college, something unusual in the town where they live. Homer and his friends made a decision to stick together even if it cost them popularity or status.

At various times in your teenage years, you will be faced with a critical choice in which you must pick loyalty to a friend or loyalty to a status within a group. If you don't have the courage to stand up for a friend when he is being picked on, you are not a true friend, and you will not experience all the blessings that true friends bring to each other. And if you can't stand up for your friend, don't expect him or others to stand up for you. Friends protect each other like a noble knight. They are loyal and courageous.

How you treat others makes a big difference in how you are treated. Who your friends are makes big difference also. Your friends will have a significant influence on your attitudes, and beliefs and behavior. They impact even your character. The Bible tells us that bad company corrupts good character, so pick your friends wisely. Don't be afraid to lovingly hold them accountable and to respectfully point them in proper directions. But also, don't be afraid to let go of friendships. You will need friendships, but you will need the right kind of friendship—that of a true friend.

Even true friends will let you down sometimes. Don't shy away from telling a friend how he hurt you or disappointed you. Be willing to forgive. Failing to talk about disappointments in your friendship, even about small things—and failing to forgive— unfortunately can end many meaningful friendships. At the same time, have the guts to apologize and seek forgiveness when you hurt a friend.

You will also need some time alone as a teenager. Don't be afraid of being alone. It doesn't mean you're weak or unpopular. Jesus often retreated from his friends and the crowd to be by himself and to pray. Don't feel like you have to fill up every minute with friends or activities, or be on a cell phone or computer all the time. You'll be a better friend—and a better person—if you cultivate the habit of being alone as well as the habits of being a true friend. Sometimes, we stay so busy with friends and scheduled activities that we neglect our inner self and our relationship with God. Spend quiet time each day in prayer, meditation and in the Bible. Spend time each day reading, thinking and relaxing. Your life will have better balance, and your friendships will be stronger as well. Good friendships depend more on the quality of time spent together than the quantity of time.

It is never too early to start seeking out true friendships. Establishing these friendships early will help prevent problems down the road. The upcoming years will be full of challenges. The journey ahead is much easier if you have some "wing men" who are willing to fly with you through the good and the bad. But perhaps most significantly, you will experience a lifetime of deep joys that true friends can bring. God built us for connection and intimacy with each other, and being a man means entering into true friendships.

Chapter 4
Questions for Reflection and Discussion

1. Think about the guys to whom you are closest. Are they true friends or shallow friends?

2. Why do you have the friends that you do? What do you look for in a friend?

3. Are any of your classmates or friends from a different background? What person from a different background can you try to build a friendship with? What can you do to build it?

4. What have you given to a friend or sacrificed for a friend? What act of service and kindness could you do for a friend this week?

5. Do you talk with your friends about deep and important and emotional issues or do you keep that hidden? What are you hiding from your friends?

6. When was the last time you had to tell a friend something that was hard or uncomfortable for him to hear? Do you have a friend right now with whom you need to have a difficult but loving conversation?

7. Do you have any friends right now who are corrupting you? Do you need to let go of any friendships?

8. Are your friends and activities keeping you too busy and consumed to have alone time with God? If so, what adjustments might you need to make to create that time?

Chapter 5

Cabin Pressure

There's one advantage to being 102. There's no peer pressure.

— Dennis Wolfberg, Comedian

My best friend is the one who brings out the best in me.

— Henry Ford, Founder of Ford Motor Company

"You're hired." Air Force fighter pilot Captain Jeremy Hansen finally heard those words from the Canadian Space Agency (CSA) on May 13, 2009, becoming one of two new Canadian astronauts.

Capt. Hansen, a pilot at 4 Wing Cold Lake, and David St-Jacques, a Quebec City doctor with a PhD in astrophysics, beat out about 5,300 hopeful applicants, going through year-long testing and evaluation to finally be the two who remained standing when the CSA culminated its third national recruitment campaign.

"It's overwhelming," said Capt. Hansen. "I'm excited, ecstatic...I'm nervous a little bit, intimidated, humbled. It's just an amazing opportunity."

Capt. Hansen and other candidates went through a number of evaluations that included medical and aptitude tests.

"One task would be fighting a fire in full fire-fighting gear, working as a team," explained Capt. Hansen. "The next test would [involve] a portion of a ship...sinking and freezing cold water...rushing in. You have to stop the leaks and patch the holes. It was physically and mentally exhausting."

Capt. Hansen credits his Air Force training for helping him realize his dream. "The Air Cadet program really enabled me to accomplish my goals," Capt. Hansen said. "It was a great basis for my life, a lot of great skills and a lot of amazing opportunities."

"I don't think I'd be in this position without my Air Force experiences," he continued. "My military flying and my fighter flying has taught me how to react to being under pressure. On a regular basis, I'm asked to perform while I'm flying a fighter jet under dynamic and stressful situations."

-story courtesy of Canada Air Force News

In the upcoming years, you will be faced with a number of difficult and stressful situations. Like Captain Hansen, you will need to rely on what you have learned in order to get through. This chapter will give you the necessary information and strategies to help you navigate through the difficulties of peer pressure. Without a plan, you will inevitably find yourself flying off course and into potential danger.

Peer pressure is social pressure by members of one's peer group to take a certain action, adopt certain values, or otherwise conform in order to be accepted.

For all the ways a true friend can enrich your life, there are many ways that "friends" can get you side-tracked. For all the great things about the teenage years, one of the most unfortunate things about the journey ahead is the overemphasis that is placed on popularity and being cool. You will feel a pressure, a pull, to be just like everybody else, to conform to what they are doing, to be the sort of person you think they will like. You will be pushed to please your buddies and classmates more than your parents or any other adult. You will care more about your looks, clothes and belongings than you did last year, and you will want your looks, clothes and belongings to be like your classmates (which will probably be based on what you see in the movies, TV, magazines and with teenagers a little older than you).

Peer pressure covers a number of areas in a young man's life. It covers more areas than you might think. Let's look at some of the pressures you will face in the upcoming years:

1 **Stress:** Dealing with pressures and stress in middle school and high school can be hard sometimes. The pressure to make friends, earn good grades, excel in sports or other activities, deal with crammed schedules, establish and maintain relationships, and navigate an occasionally difficult home life can feel overwhelming at times. Dealing with all of this can mess with your self-esteem, outlook on life, mood, and health. The next thing you know you're feeling stressed or worse.

Basically, my problem was attributed to stress more than anything. I don't know what that does and I guess doctors can tell you that there's chemicals that build up in your system when you go through a lot of stress and constant stress.

– Mike Ditka, Former Chicago Bears Coach

2 **In Crowd:** During high school you may hear your friends, parents or even a coach tell you to "just be yourself" – but what does that really mean? Knowing who you are and what you believe in is important. Recognizing the influences in your life (both good and bad) makes it easier for you to make important choices about who to hang out with and whether or not to try drugs or alcohol.

I firmly believe that respect is a lot more important, and a lot greater, than popularity.

– Dr. J, Julius Erving, Hall of Fame Basketball Player

3 **Image:** These days you can hardly turn a few pages in a magazine or sit through a movie without getting flooded with images of the "perfect" guy or girl. It's a bit unrealistic to think that life is truly like that. Sometimes girls wrongly believe that being super skinny will make them more appealing. For guys, it may be about looking bigger or stronger. Look around – there are all kinds of people in the world. And nearly everyone has something about themselves they don't really like. So body image is your own idea of what your body looks like. And how you feel about yourself has a lot to do with how you see yourself and your body.

The image is one thing and the human being is another. It's very hard to live up to an image, put it that way.

– Elvis Presley, Rock and Roll Legend

4 **Opposite Sex:** Pressure for guys can be intense when it comes to sex. Sometimes it might seem like everyone in high school (and on TV) is talking about who "does" and who "doesn't." Unfortunately, some teens feel that they have to hook up to keep dating someone or to be accepted. That's pretty sad. You will be pressured by your friends and girls your age.

5 **Drugs and Alcohol:** There's a lot of "information" floating around the Web about drugs and alcohol. Some of it is even misinformation spreading by word-of-mouth. The movies, music and other media don't always accurately portray the risks of use either. You will, if you haven't already, encounter occasions to use alcohol, tobacco and drugs.

It's so easy for a kid to join a gang, to do drugs... we should make it that easy to be involved in football and academics.

– Snoop Dogg, Rapper

6 **Control:** There are many ways that young people tease (or bully) each other, even if they don't realize it at the time. Bullying can be direct attacks like punching, teasing, name-calling, or taunting someone online. It can also include spreading rumors or encouraging others to exclude someone. You may even feel guilty if you're pressured by your friends to join in on the taunting when you know it's not right. If someone is encouraging you to pick on someone else, stand your ground and don't take part. In most cases you'll find that when a bully doesn't have an audience, he (or she) may be less likely to keep it up. Speak up and defend the person being picked on.

If you bully somebody face to face, and they get upset, you see them cry and be hurt. When it's over the Internet, you can't see the emotional reaction and go along thinking it's no big deal.

– Robin Kowalski, Author

*Information Courtesy of Above the Influence.

Even if you don't realize it, peers influence your life, just by spending time with you. You learn from them, and they learn from you. It's only human nature to listen to and learn from other people in your age group. You will have many chances for joining some of your peers in ridiculing a classmate, looking at pornography, and watching the wrong sorts of movies. You will have opportunities to explore sexual relationships with girls. You will be tempted to do all of these things not simply to show your independence and that you are becoming a young man, but because you believe that your peers will like you more and find you cooler if you do these things.

What is peer pressure? Peer pressure is the push you feel that seems to be forcing you in that direction. It's powerful, and everyone feels it, even adults. But it is most powerful during the next few years of your life.

Understanding the real cause of peer pressure can help you to avoid some of its traps and relieve some of your anxieties. Let us tell you what psychologists tell us. At its most basic level, conformity and peer pressure mostly relate to the insecurities and inferiorities we feel. Satan wants us to think poorly of ourselves and to forget that we have incredible value and worth because God created us and redeems us. We think we are not attractive, talented, or smart. We therefore don't feel good about ourselves, even if on the outside we appear happy, confident, successful and handsome to everyone else. If you could hear the thoughts of many teenagers, you'd probably be surprised at their low regard for themselves. So many things are in the process of changing in a teenager (body, mind, friends, identity and values, to name a few) that they often feel very uncomfortable and unsure of themselves. It's often an awkward time when you don't feel especially attractive, when you get cut from teams and realize, maybe for the first time, that there are people more talented than you are. You may think you are too skinny or too fat, that your voice is too deep or too squeaky, that you're uncomfortable with girls, and that everyone is staring at that zit on your face. The early years of adolescence, for all of its adventure, bring discomfort and disorientation, and many teenagers hide these things by trying to be just like everyone else. No one wants to stand out.

And as you begin to feel the urge to break away a bit from your childhood relationship with your parents, it is also natural that you will seek closer relationships with your friends. They will become a bigger factor in your decision making. They will be with you when you are faced with a big decision related to peer pressure.

When the time comes for you to make these big decisions, remember the following:

- ♱ Take as long as you need just to think about whether you want to do it.
- ♱ Don't make a quick decision because your friends are pushing you to.
- ♱ List all your options, and think about the consequences of each.
- ♱ Know who is asking you to do something. If the person is not your friend, you should really consider what they want you to do, but if you know, trust and respect this person, then you might seriously consider what they ask.

Stop for a minute and consider the influence your peers or friends are having on your life. How important is it that you please them? How important is it that they like you? How many of your thoughts focus on what they probably think about you and how you can fit in with them? For most teenagers, the influence is great, and the thoughts are frequent, sometimes nearly constant.

But does it really matter if we want to be just like our friends? It depends on what your friends and the group are doing. It depends on their values and standards. And it depends on the topic. We suppose it's not a big deal if everyone is wearing the same clothing style, whereas polluting your body with cigarettes like them is a much different matter. A good question to ask yourself is this: do I need to do this (whatever "this" is; fill in the blank) to gain recognition in the eyes of my peers?

There are both positive and negative peer pressure. Unfortunately, during the teenage years, there is usually a lot more of the negative variety than there is the positive type. What does negative peer pressure do?

- ✚ It can cause you to make poor decisions that harm yourself and others.
- ✚ It can cause you to make decisions that change your life forever.
- ✚ It can cause you to make a deadly decision.
- ✚ It limits your ability to be a leader. Conformists can't be leaders because they are like everyone else.
- ✚ It can short-circuit you from growing into the man God wants you to be.
- ✚ It leads you away from God.

Do not conform any longer to the pattern of this world, but be transformed by the renewing of your mind.

– Romans 12:2

If you are a follower of Christ, you are called to lead a different life than how the world tells you to live. Your behavior and customs are to be unique. You are to follow Christ and God's instructions for your life. God's instructions are to be deeply planted in your mind. God's Word and the Holy Spirit renew your mind; they change the way you see the world, how you think about the world and, therefore, how you live in this world. In Colossians 3:2, Paul tells us to "set your minds on things above, not on earthly things." Studying the Scriptures allows us to renew our minds and view the world differently than many people do.

What about you? Do you think about the world differently than the way the "crowd" does? Do you have different values than the ones that come across on most TV shows and movies? If you think about the world differently, that's an important and great starting point for resisting negative peer pressure, but you will be tempted anyway.

We will still be tempted to follow the behaviors, values and patterns of the world. Jesus was tempted by Satan in the desert. He was offered the things that so often tempt us: power, splendor, popularity and possessions. He stayed firm and focused on worshipping and serving the Lord. His mind had been renewed.

Know that you will be tempted over the next few years. Know that these temptations (and the sins to which they lead) will be much more enticing and exciting than the temptations of your childhood. What are some examples of situations in which you will face peer pressure?

Here are some common ones:

- Being cruel to a classmate (to their face or behind their back).
- Tearing down someone's reputation and gossiping (including calling a classmate gay or something else hurtful).
- Talking inappropriately about girls, especially about their bodies.
- Using inappropriate language.
- Drinking, dipping, smoking and using other drugs.
- Looking at pornography.
- Watching inappropriate movies.
- Cheating.
- Vandalizing property.
- Engaging in stupid, risky behaviors.
- Disrespecting your parents, including lying to them.
- Making up things about a girl.
- Cyberbullying someone through Facebook, Twitter, My Space or some form of social media.

What are these situations likely to look like? Here are a few examples:

 Scenario #1: It's Friday night; you and one of your friends are spending the night with another buddy from your class. These guys are two of your best friends. It's about midnight—you've been watching TV, playing video games and now you're just talking. At some point, you start talking about other classmates. Your best friend starts making fun of Bill. "He's a loser." Or "He thinks he's so cool." Or "No girl is ever going to like him." Or "He's gay." Or "Do you know what so and so said about him?" Your friends are laughing at how pathetic they think this guy is. What do you do? Why?

 Scenario #2: You've made the baseball team, and as you and the other outfielders are standing out in left field at a practice, one of them pulls some dip out of his back pocket. He puts some in his mouth and then passes the can of dip around. Just in case anyone is hesitant, he tells everyone that no one will be able to see them with it, that the coach is hundreds of feet away, and that the coach dips also. He hands the dip can to you. What do you do? Why?

 Scenario #3: One of your friends at school is having a party. It's a great party—lots of girls, good music, your closest friends are there and his "cool" parents are, of course, home but they're kind of out of the way. They're upstairs, and they don't know what is happening. They assume that middle school students would never think about drinking or smoking. At 10:00, your buddy Tucker shows you and two girls what he's got in his backpack: a bottle of Jack Daniels whiskey. He pours some Jack into his Coke. "Now this is the joy of cola," he says, and he pours some for Lauren and Sally. Lauren is this girl that you and about a dozen other guys are quite interested in. Jackson reaches for your cup as he prepares to pour some Jack Daniels into your drink. What do you do? Why?

Scenario #4: You and three of your friends are at the movies. Sitting near you all, some guys from a rival school start tossing popcorn in your hair during the movie. One of them "spills" a coke onto the back of your friend's shirt. Your friends exchange a few ugly words with those guys. One of your friends says we'll beat them up after the movie. Your other friend agrees. They look at you and ask you if you're in also. What do you do? Why?

 Scenario #5: Your family, along with some other families and teenagers you know, are on spring break together at the beach. The parents decide that they will all go to dinner together, and they leave you and the other teenagers with some money to order pizza and hang out at the beach. The parents say to be safe and to be back at the condos by 11:00. Everyone is hanging out at the beach, and when the sun goes down, two of the other teenagers bring a case of beer. They start handing out beers and then some pot. What do you do? Why?

 Scenario #6: It's a Friday night in your sophomore year. Your high school has just won the football game, and you and your three closest friends decide to get in Tom's car and just drive around for a while. Tom is the only one with his driver's license. Tom eventually pulls into a deserted parking lot. He pops the trunk to reveal a case of Budweiser that he's probably taken from his parents' refrigerator in the garage. They've always got it stocked. Before you know it, he's chugged three beers and is sipping on a fourth. Your friends are drinking as well. It's 10:30, and you are due home in 30 minutes. What do you do? Why?

 Scenario #7: You've just taken the big history test, and you're having lunch with two of your good friends. They take the test later that afternoon. Jack tells you he didn't have a chance to study very much for the test. Paul needs to make a good grade or he may be suspended from the basketball team for low grades, and his parents may ground him. "What's on the test?" one of them asks. "Help us out." What do you do? Why?

So what are some practical things you can do to limit your vulnerability to peer pressure and to make the sort of decisions that are pleasing to God? Here are some principles and tips. As you'll see, most of them involve making decisions and preparing yourself for the pressures before you actually experience them. Most successful coaches will tell you that games are won because of all of the preparation and practice before the actual game.

 Get your worth from God.

Knowing that God created you, loves you and is willing to forgive you through Jesus Christ frees you up to have a deep sense of value and worth that is impossible to truly have otherwise. Lots of people try to use worldly things to fill up a hole they have inside about who they are. Only God can fill that hole or emptiness, and until you understand and accept that, you will also be very vulnerable to worldly conformity and peer pressure.

 Get advice and encouragement from your parents.

Tell them the types of peer pressure you are facing. Their wisdom and encouragement can be helpful. Rehearse with them what you'll say in difficult situations. Also, use them to bail you out of parties where there is drinking and drug use. Work out a plan and message so they'll know you need to be picked up. This might include creating a type of code that your parents will understand when you call. Talk to them about escape plans from tricky situations. You can even blame them for not letting you go to certain parties by asking them to ground you for a night if that's what you need to do to say no to going.

 Have a friend who holds you accountable.

In your battle with peer pressure, friends make a huge difference. Find at least one friend with whom you will share a commitment about the sort of choices you will make as a teenager. Ask him to make these same commitments to you, and then hold each other accountable. If one of you starts to stray from the right path, it is the responsibility of the other friend to point this out in a firm yet loving way.

 Stand up for each other.

Having just one person do the same thing makes a huge difference. Two or three people together saying we won't drink or ridicule often changes the behavior of the whole crowd. Proverbs 27:7 says:

As iron sharpens iron, so one man sharpens another.

– Proverbs 27:7

Good friends will sharpen you: your thinking, your actions, and your values. They will also help you grow spiritually.

 Choose your friends carefully.

While it is important to encourage straying friends to make appropriate choices, there are some times when it is wise to break off certain friendships, either temporarily or permanently. If your friends are dragging you down the wrong path, then they are not true friends, and you should find new ones. I Corinthians 15:33 tells us that bad company corrupts good character. Have the courage to let go of friends. Also, know that it is normal and natural that who your friends are normally changes as you move from elementary school to middle school and then again to high school.

 Ask an older person to serve as a mentor.

As adults, we both meet on a regular basis with older men who serve as mentors to us. They are wise, Godly men who have a set of life experiences that we do not yet have. We both also serve as mentors to a few teenagers. We talk about their grades, peer pressure, girlfriends, sports, spiritual growth, work ethic, friends and relationships with their families. They ask us questions, and we give advice. We can offer them a perspective on life that they don't yet have. We encourage each of you to ask an older person to be a mentor to you. We think you will be blessed by it.

 Decide in advance what you will say and do in situations involving negative peer pressure.

In the next chapter, we'll talk specifically about drugs and alcohol and other situations in which you feel a strong pressure to make a poor choice. If you have not already decided in advance what you will say and do, we can almost assure you that you will make the wrong decision in the heat of the moment. Know what you will say. Practice it with a parent, friend and your mentor. That way, it won't be as hard when the real test comes.

 Practice saying no to peer pressure now.

You are already feeling some types of peer pressure. Start building your skill now of saying no to negative peer pressure. If your friends realize now that you are strong and secure enough to say no to negative peer pressure, they may be less likely to tempt you later. If they do tempt you down the road, your "no" won't be so hard to say, and it won't be shocking to them.

 Let go of the need to be cool and popular.

Being a follower of Jesus Christ will not always make you cool and popular. In fact, John tells us in I John 3:13 that the world may hate you. Wow, that doesn't seem very good. But God gives us a far greater joy and promise than worldly popularity.

Do not love the world or anything in the world. If anyone loves the world, the love of the Father is not in him. For everyone in the world—the cravings of sinful man, the lust of his eyes, and the boasting of what he has and does—comes not from the Father but from the world. The world and its desires pass away, but the man who does the will of God lives forever.

– I John 2:15-16

 10 Be yourself.

God created you exactly the way you are. Accept that. Accept your differences. Rejoice in them. Don't pretend to be someone you are not. It dishonors God, and it takes a lot of your energy to be an actor. Don't invent a personality for yourself. Being a fake is tiring and will eventually drive people away anyway. If someone can't accept you for who you are, then you should seek other friends.

 11 Don't tease others or stand by silently when it happens.

Over the next few years, you will probably see more guys making fun of people. It will probably be directed at a certain group of guys or girls. Much of it is an attempt to fit in and be cool. Most of it will be more verbal than physical. Don't underestimate the pain that you and your classmates can cause to an individual who may seem like he is handling it OK. Don't let things like this happen. Real men—noble knights—care for the weak. It can take just one person standing up for a ridiculed classmate to change the whole dynamic. Be that person. Be a leader.

As with all of the teenage issues you will face, if you have the finished product in mind—the sort of man God designed you to be—all of these things will fall into place as they should. Reflect back on the virtues of manhood that we began this book with. If you understand what it means to be a true friend, you won't fall prey to the superficial things that most people think constitutes friendship. If you have a heroic purpose for your life, you'll see how silly so much of the teenage issues are, and you'll see how easily it can sidetrack the bigger purpose of your life. If you seek out and embrace bold adventures for your life, you'll see that so many of the typical teenage "adventures" are shallow and boring by comparison. If you are a servant leader, you'll understand that going against the crowd is leadership, and that by setting a Godly example, you are serving your friends. Similarly, if you are a noble knight, you will protect and defend your community of friends. You will be motivated to exert positive peer pressure based on the sort of moral community God wants for us.

If you can resist negative peer pressure now, you will as a man be more likely to resist the pressure to manage your image. Many men spend much of their time and energy in trying to create an image that will impress others. It's almost always an image conformed to the things of this world, and though it looks good on the outside, it usually leads to hollowness on the inside.

Resisting peer pressure is not easy. You will need God's help. Ask Him to give you the wisdom and courage to make the sort of choices He wants for you. And remember this last bit of perspective: boys do the easy thing, but men do the right thing!

Chapter 5
Questions for Reflection and Discussion

1. Do you spend a lot of time wondering what your classmates and friends and other people think about you? If so, why?

2. What types of peer pressure have you already faced? What do you think the hardest peer pressure to resist will be for you?

3. Are you practicing saying no to certain types of peer pressure right now?

4. Do you have a friend who will stand up with you and hold you accountable for making good decisions? Have you already talked to him? If you don't have a person like that in place already, who would be a good person to ask?

5. Is there someone at least ten years older than you from whom you seek advice on a regular basis? If not, who might that person be?

6. Is what is cool with your classmates and friends cool with God?

7. Are you doing anything now to renew your mind—to see the world the way God sees it? What can you do this week to renew your mind?

8. Have you faced situations when you had to choose between loyalty to a friend and loyalty to the group? What did you do?

9. Have you decided and written out exactly what you will say and do in situations involving negative peer pressure? Have you practiced it?

10. Are you ok if you're not considered cool? Why or why not?

11. Have you created am image of yourself for others to see that is not the real you? If so, what is that image, and why did you do it?

12. What does it mean to be yourself?

Chapter 6

Potential Crash Landing

If you must drink and drive, drink Pepsi.

— Author Unknown, As Seen on a Bumper Sticker

———————— ⇟ ————————

Young people can get very discouraged and get hooked on drugs or on alcohol because of problems they perceive as insurmountable.

— Maureen Forrester, Author

———————— ⇟ ————————

In November 2009, Yves Rossy, a 50 year old Swiss adventurer and former fighter pilot, attempted to soar from Morocco to Spain on jet-powered wings. His mission failed mid-flight, and he ditched safely into the Atlantic on Wednesday after hitting turbulence and clouds so thick he could not tell if he was flying up or down. Rossy took off from Tangiers, but about four minutes into the flight, he hit turbulence and entered clouds that he described as beautiful but disorienting because he could not see and had no reference points.

Eventually he found himself wobbling and dropping at up to 180 miles per hour until he was just 2,500 feet above the water. At that rate he would have hit it in about 20 seconds.

"So the sea comes very fast," he said. "Unstable, at this height, there is no playing anymore. So I throw away my wing and opened my parachute."

The upcoming years will be filled with temptations that at first will seem exciting but can often be disorienting. We do not want you to be forced to be pull the chute at the last minute. This chapter will deal with two big temptations that you will be facing soon. Pay close attention. What might seem harmless to you might disorient you and throw you off course.

One of the greatest temptations you will face as a teenager is to drink, smoke and use other drugs. It's natural to be curious about those things and have lots of questions:

- ♣ What does beer taste like, and why do so many people drink?
- ♣ My parents drink, or at least some adults I know do, so how can there be anything wrong with drinking?
- ♣ What's it like to be high? Will life be more fun if I'm drunk or stoned or on drugs?
- ♣ Won't I be more of a man, or at least not a child, if I drink and smoke?
- ♣ Will I feel and experience things more intensely if I snort cocaine or Ritalin or take ecstasy?
- ♣ Won't I fit in with my friends more easily, and won't I be more relaxed with girls, if I drink and smoke pot?
- ♣ Won't I be cooler with a cigarette dangling out of my mouth?

You'll wrestle with these questions soon if you haven't already, and you'll have opportunities for drinking, smoking and using drugs. A classmate will sneak a bottle of vodka to a party at a friend's house; he'll pour shots into soft drinks. A classmate will tell you to come to the bathroom or the parking lot at the school dance to smoke a joint. You'll spend the night at a friend's house, and he'll suggest that you get some beers from the refrigerator in the garage. You and your buddies will meet a few girls at the movie theater, and they'll pull out some cigarettes from their purses and suggest that you all go behind the theater to smoke. You'll meet a group of friends on the beach at night, and two of them will bring a case of beer. Some of your classmates, probably even some of your friends, will drink, smoke and use other drugs in the upcoming months and years. What about you? What will you do? We'll talk about all of these questions and temptations in this chapter, but let's start with alcohol.

We start with alcohol because it is, in many cases, one of the first temptations you will face. Research shows that alcohol is the drug of choice among youth. Many young people are experiencing the consequences of drinking too much at too early an age. As a result, underage drinking is a leading public health problem in this country. We will address more specifics later on in the chapter.

But first, we'll tell you a story to illustrate the relationship between alcohol, boys and men.

Imagine this. One of your best friends has a go-cart and a big back yard. After school and on the weekends, the two of you love to ride that go-cart around all over his yard. Of course, you drive it as fast as it will go. You zip around trees and make sharp turns. Sometimes, you spin out in the yard. You pretend you're NASCAR drivers. You love the speed—the wind blowing in your hair—and the power of driving an engine.

Now pretend for a moment that you and your friend wish the go-cart would go faster, so the two of you secretly take it down to the local BMW dealership and talk to the manager and ask him to install in the go-cart a V-12, 300 horsepower engine—the same engine found in many BMW's. Suppose for a moment that he sells you that engine (you tell him to charge it to your parents) and that he installs it. Picture the little go-cart with that huge engine with all of its power. Think how fast you could accelerate from 0-60 miles per hour. Think how fast you could go. Could you go 100 mph? 120 mph? 180 mph? You figure that since the go-cart is so little and the engine so big, you could probably go even faster than the much heavier BMW could go.

So you and your buddy sneak the suped-up go-cart to his house and, when you guys determine his mom won't be looking, you get ready to ride it. Of course, you tell yourselves, we will drive safely. You crank the engine and get ready to go for a much more exhilarating go-cart ride than what you guys are used to.

What do you think would happen to you and your friend?

You would probably injure or kill yourselves. You would barely touch the accelerator and it would go so fast that you would lose control and flip it. Or maybe you would start out ok for just a little bit, but when you hit that first curve, you would flip it because you would be going faster than the aerodynamics or structure of the car could handle on a curve. Or maybe you would be ok for a minute or two, but when you were ready to stop the go-cart near the garage, you would be going too fast, and the breaks would be too flimsy to stop the little go-cart short of the brick wall. We feel certain that you would crash the go-cart in one of these three ways or in some other way that doesn't end well. With the temptation of a powerful engine and some freedom from a parent watching, probably no boy or teenager would have the self-control and self-discipline to drive the go-cart slowly enough to be safe.

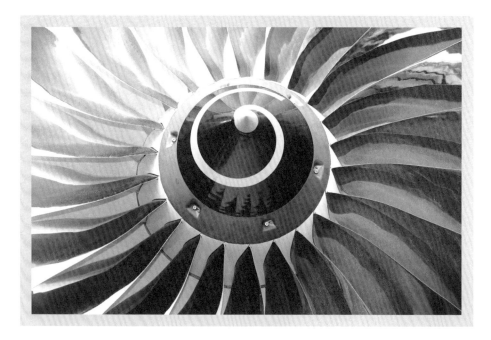

Now this exact same V-12, 300 horsepower engine is usually very safe in a BMW driven by a responsible adult, but it is dangerous, destructive and deadly if placed in a smaller vehicle like a go-cart.

What is the meaning of this story? As a teenager, you are a go-cart, and putting alcohol in your body is like putting a V-12 engine in a go-cart. It's a formula for disaster. When you are twenty-one or older, you are much more like a car that is designed to accommodate safely a V-12 engine in most situations. Alcohol, used in certain ways by certain adults, can be acceptable and safe. Why is this? Because adult bodies and minds are very different from teenage bodies and minds, just as go-carts and cars are very different from one another. As a teenager, your brain is still forming neural connections, and the part of the brain that handles judgment and decisions is a long way from being fully formed. Your bodies are still developing and growing. You are more impulsive and less wise and experienced. The teenage mind and body is like the go-cart in that it doesn't have enough weight and aerodynamic sophistication to keep it from flipping when it is going fast. It doesn't have computer chips to adjust the engine, headlights to see far ahead, a good breaking system, airbags to protect, and so forth. Most adults have those things.

Drinking continues to be widespread among adolescents, as shown by nationwide surveys as well as studies in smaller populations. Nearly four out of ten students have consumed alcohol at least once by the end of eighth grade and slightly more than seven out of ten students have done so by the end of high school. That is, 39% of eighth grade students, 58% of tenth graders, and 72% of twelfth graders report they have tried alcohol at least once in their lifetime.

Source- University of Michigan, Monitoring the Future, 2008

God knows that as a teenager, you and alcohol or any drugs are a bad mix. He knows that they will stunt your growth, harm your development, lower your achievement and hurt your relationships. He loves you and wants what is best for you. That is why He wants you never to drink in your teenage years and perhaps only drink as an adult under certain circumstances. God does permit some types of drinking by adults. Let's look at what the Bible says about drinking:

- ♣ Genesis 27:28: Isaac says to Jacob: "May God give you of heaven's dew and of earth's richness—an abundance of grain and new wine."

♣ Deuteronomy 14:26: "Use the silver to buy whatever you like: cattle, sheep, wine or other fermented drink."

♣ Psalm 104:14-15: "He makes grass grow for the cattle and plants for man to cultivate—bringing forth food from the earth: wine that gladdens the heart of man, oil to make his face shine, and bread that sustains his heart."

♣ Proverbs 3:9-10: "Honor the Lord with your wealth, with the first-fruits of all your crops; then your barns will be filled to overflowing and your vats will brim over with new wine."

♣ John 2:1-11: Jesus turns water into wine at wedding in Cana.

Bible-believing Christians can apply these verses differently and make different decisions about alcohol, and we very much respect those differing views. However, getting drunk—which means drinking more than just a little bit (say, more than 1-2 drinks for most adults, depending on a person's size, weight, and a few other factors)—is a sin and brings on all sorts of problems. Getting drunk is a misuse, or an abuse, of a gift from God. One of Satan's top tricks is to take a gift from God and encourage us to pervert it. Let's see what the Bible says about drinking too much.

Do not join those who drink too much wine or gorge themselves on meat, for drunkards and gluttons become poor, and drowsiness clothes them in rags.

– Proverbs 23:20

Do not get drunk on wine, which leads to debauchery. Instead, be filled with the Spirit.

– Ephesians 5:18

So adults who can legally enjoy God's gift of a drink should only do so in moderation. God cautions us that drinking more than a very little bit leads to a host of problems, and He also tells us that even for adults, there are certain times when they should not drink (for instance, if it will be a stumbling block to other people; in other words, if an adult's drinking somehow encourages someone else to head down a dangerous path). He also tells us that everything that is permissible for us to do is not always a good idea. So all adults should be careful and moderate in their drinking, but they should also consider whether or not it is advisable for them to drink at all in the first place. So when you turn twenty-one, it doesn't mean you should drink; it means you can drink, having first carefully considered your own circumstances and those around you to see if it is a good idea. Many adults, including many Christians, make a wise and disciplined decision not to drink at all.

Before we look at the problems associated with drinking, and look specifically at teenage drinking, let's consider what drinking actually does. If you are like us when we were your age, you are probably wondering why so many people drink. There must be something good—or at least powerful—about it:

1 Drinking relaxes you. Some men will say that it "takes the edge off after a stressful day at work." Many people feel a little more comfortable in social settings during or after they've had a drink. It slows down the heart rate, dulls the senses, and can create a warm feeling inside. Drinking to feel more comfortable around other people is a crutch that may, in the short run, make you feel a little more relaxed and give you a superficial and fake confidence, but in the long run, it causes you not to develop as fully as a person and in your relationships with other people.

2 Drinking lowers or eliminates certain inhibitions you may normally have. You become much more impulsive and irrational when you are drinking. You may find it easier to initiate and have a conversation with a girl, but you are also more likely to say something stupid or offensive to her. You are more likely to argue and fight, to vandalize or steal, and to be rude and crude. You are more likely to be sexually active and aggressive with a girl. Most teenagers who have sex have been drinking. You are more likely to smoke marijuana, snort cocaine, or take pills. Your instincts and impulses (many of which are not good) take over as your thoughts and values take a back seat.

3 Drinking makes teenagers feel more grown up. It's quite normal during adolescence to start to see yourself as more of an adult, and it's natural to want to experience grown-up things. You see adults sipping wine in restaurants or relaxing with a scotch on the sofa. A beer and a ballgame look like a good fit for men, so you want to experience those adult things also. After all, you've outgrown legos, G-rated movies and action figures, you're as tall as your mom, and you have the same shoe size and wear the same deodorant as your dad. "Shouldn't you then be able to share a drink with them?" you think to yourself. "Why do adults drink?" you wonder.

4 Drinking may complement the type of food adults are ordering. It may bring out the flavor of certain foods. A glass of red wine may intensify the taste of a filet mignon. A glass of white wine may bring out the flavor of seafood. Beer, though, actually deadens the taste buds. Speaking of taste, alcohol of any type is an acquired taste, meaning that the first time it is drunk, it does not taste very good. Many drinks with alcohol have a bitter flavor and may sting or burn a little bit at first as they go down. As an individual drinks alcohol many times, he gradually comes to tolerate and then even enjoy and appreciate the taste.

5 There are medical reasons for an adult to drink. Some doctors encourage adults with certain types of heart problems to drink a glass of red wine several times a week.

Three basic categories of alcohol:

* Beer
* Wine
* Hard liquor

Alcohol Content: what is it and why is important?

- Alcohol content is a standard measure of how much alcohol (ethanol) is contained in an alcoholic beverage.
- Alcohol content is expressed as a percentage of volume or weight.
- Drinks have differing alcohol contents, with beer having the least and hard liquor the most.
- The greater the alcohol content, the greater the effect on the body.
- A very small amount of hard liquor may have the same or greater effect as a 12-ounce beer.
- The less you weigh, the longer since you've eaten, and the less frequently you drink, the greater effect the alcohol will have on your body.

Whether it's a Budweiser, shot of Jack Daniels, or glass of red or white wine, teenage drinking is wrong and problematic in several ways. It violates the law (you have to be twenty-one to consume alcohol in the United States), and Romans 13:1-7 says we are to obey all civil laws unless they prevent us from worshipping Him. God recognizes the value of laws that promote an orderly, safe and moral society. There is nothing inconsistent about worshipping God and not drinking if you are under twenty-one. Therefore, God does not want you to drink as a teenager.

If it is against the law for a guy your age to drink, then why do teenagers drink?

"Matthew, age sixteen, was an average student who sometimes earned B's and even an A occasionally when a subject grabbed his intelligent but often apathetic mind. He was a nice kid, and really didn't have any "problems." He was a good big brother to twelve-year old Katie and went to church regularly.

Matthew came to see me for counseling two days after being admitted to the emergency room for alcohol poisoning. He had a blood alcohol level of .379—almost five times the legal limit in most states and a potentially lethal level. Matthew's parents had no idea that their son even drank. He was lucky that he didn't die or suffer any organ damage. The American Psychological Association defines binge drinking as consuming five alcoholic drinks in an hour. Matthew thought he had probably consumed sixteen shots in about a ninety-minute timeframe. In my conversations with him I asked him what his intention was when he was getting ready to go out that night. He told me that he needed to show his friends that he could keep up with the other guys. He said, 'My popularity was riding on that night.'"

-John E. Davis in Extreme Pursuit

Matthew and many guys like him do things like this because they feel as if this is their chance to be popular. The chase for popularity is one of several reasons why teenagers drink. Here are some others:

- To make them feel good.
- To forget their problems.
- To take a risk.
- To get rid of anger or frustration.

Alcohol abuse and alcohol dependence are not only adult problems — they also affect a significant number of adolescents and young adults between the ages of twelve and twenty, even though drinking under the age of twenty-one is illegal. Excessive drinking, especially as a teenager, creates a number of dangers.

Your judgment will be compromised. You may take dangerous risks that normally you would have the good sense to avoid. You may pass out at some point. You will possibly throw up. If you throw up after you have passed out, you could choke on your vomit and die. You can get alcohol poisoning and die. The next morning, you will have a hangover. You will probably have a terrible headache and upset stomach and feel dehydrated, tired, gross and grumpy.

Drinking is dangerous in that some people will become alcoholics if they ever begin drinking. Alcoholism is a disease in which your body must have alcohol once it has had some. If you know that alcoholism runs in your family, you may be predisposed to be an alcoholic, so it's probably a good idea not to drink ever. Ask your parents if any blood relative in your family is an alcoholic.

Drinking can damage the liver and brain and lead to death. Recent brain scans comparing young adults who drank as teenagers and those who did not show noticeable differences in the development and health of the brain. Recent brain research confirms that significant changes are taking place in the brain all through the teenage and early adult years. So for the full and healthy development of your brain, don't drink as a teenager.

Drinking will cause you to make a bunch of stupid (and sometimes life-changing) choices. Because drinking impairs your judgment, you are much more likely to take drugs, engage in vandalism or other criminal behavior and make poor choices with a girl. There are significant consequences for under-age drinking and for those stupid things you might do under the influence of alcohol. You can get kicked out of school and go to jail, among other things. A criminal record from underage drinking can keep you out of certain colleges or jobs as an adult. You can damage your relationship with your parents, friends and God.

Combining drinking with driving, even if you or the driver are not drunk, can be deadly. Alcohol slows the reactions and impairs judgment, and even a slight miscalculation in a car traveling 40 mph can be fatal. Car accidents are the #1 killer of teens, and many of them involve alcohol. Never drink and drive, and never ride with someone under the influence of alcohol. Don't fall to the temptation to ride with a driver who is probably not drunk or will probably drive carefully.

We suggest that you and your parents talk about an agreement that if you are in a situation where you have been drinking and are expected to drive home, or another person has been drinking and he or she is the expected driver, that you will call your parent(s) and they will come pick you up, no matter what the time or circumstances are.

You won't just be tempted with alcohol. Tobacco is an early and frequent teenage temptation. You may think that smoking a cigarette or cigar or dipping or chewing (putting tobacco in your cheek or gums) isn't a big deal. Most teenage boys underestimate the dangers and harm of tobacco. Tobacco leafs contain a drug called nicotine that is quickly absorbed into the bloodstream. While it is commonly believed that smoking relaxes you, the nicotine raises your heartbeat and blood pressure and causes the release of a hormone that creates physiological stress. The nicotine is as addictive as heroin or cocaine, meaning that once you start using it, you may not ever be able to quit. Also, once you get started, your body gets used to the chemical effect, so the body needs growing amounts of nicotine to achieve the effect it has grown accustomed to and is intensely craving.

Dangers of smoking:

- ♣ It can stunt your development
- ♣ It causes disease
- ♣ It stains your teeth
- ♣ It makes your breath stink
- ♣ It causes wrinkles and coughs and ulcers
- ♣ It reduces your stamina and immune system

When your body doesn't have the nicotine it is addicted to, it makes you irritable, anxious, tired, and nauseated, as well as have headaches and have trouble sleeping. That sounds miserable.

Why do people smoke?

- ♣ Peer pressure plays a factor. You want to fit in.
- ♣ A lot of teenage boys start smoking because they are stressed and think that smoking will relax them or give them an escape.
- ♣ Some smoke because it's a way to show they aren't a child, or they want to rebel against their parents.
- ♣ Some are just bored and see it as something adventuresome to do.

The good news is that if you can resist the pressure and shallow reasons to smoke for just a few years, you will almost surely never smoke. About 90% of smokers began smoking as a teenager. Adults don't start smoking; they started as teenagers and have not been able to quit, even though nearly all of them want to quit and probably have even tried to. It is easier never to start than it is to stop.

If you smoke, you are three times more likely to drink, eight times more likely to use marijuana, and twenty-two times more likely to use cocaine. Tobacco is often referred to as a gateway drug, meaning that if you start with tobacco, it is quite possible you won't stop there. It is a gateway on a journey toward other drugs.

Teenagers abuse a variety of drugs, both legal and illegal. Legally available drugs include the following:

- ♣ Painkillers are drugs commonly prescribed for pain and are only legally available by prescription. Painkiller abuse can be dangerous, even deadly, with too high a dose or when taken with other drugs, like alcohol. Short-term effects of painkiller abuse may include lack of energy, inability to concentrate, nausea and vomiting, and apathy. Significant doses of painkillers can cause breathing problems. When abused, painkillers can be addictive. Brand names include Vicodin, Tylenol with Codeine, OxyContin, and Percocet.

- ♣ Depressants, or downers, are prescribed to treat a variety of health conditions including anxiety and panic attacks, tension, severe stress reactions and sleep disorders. Also referred to as sedatives and tranquilizers, depressants can slow normal brain function. Health risks related to depressant abuse include loss of coordination, respiratory depression, dizziness due to lowered blood pressure, slurred speech, poor concentration, feelings of confusion and in extreme cases, coma and possible death. Brand names include Klonopin, Nembutal, Soma, Ambien, Valium, and Xanax.

- ♣ Inhalants are fumes from glues, aerosols, and solvents. Many teenagers assume that inhaling (breathing in) common household items can't be a big deal, so they sniff things from cans, from bags, or soak them in rags that they put in their mouths. These include things like glue, paint thinner, hair spray, spray paints, cleaning fluids, and gasoline. While it may cause temporary happiness and confusion, the toxics can cause headaches, loss of hearing and smell, and immediate death.

♣ Over-the-counter cough, cold, sleep and diet medications are abused by some people when they extract the DMX ingredient to have an "out-of-body" experience. Excessive DMX can result in a loss of motor control and can cause hallucinations, as well as fever, seizures, irregular heartbeat and brain damage.

The most commonly used illegal drugs are:

♣ Marijuana (pot)- It is usually smoked in what is called a joint. Marijuana affects your mood, coordination, sense of time and short-term memory. Moods may swing from happy to drowsy, and the user may experience some hallucinations. A lot of teenagers use marijuana because it may provide a temporary good feeling and make it easier to deal with or escape some of their stresses.

♣ Stimulants (cocaine, crack, and speed)- Cocaine is a powder from the dried leaves of the plant coca. When heated, it crackles and is called crack. Cocaine is snorted in the nose, while crack is smoked. Cocaine is a stimulant that shocks the central nervous system and thus produces a 15-30 minute intense high and feeling of power. It also can cause the individual to stop breathing or have a heart attack. It is intensely addictive.

♣ LSD (acid or doses)- Usually it is licked off a small square of paper and is a colorless and odorless chemical that changes your mood and makes you hallucinate. Users report perceiving bizarre colors and sounds and losing sense of time. They also experience panic attacks and frightening delusions and demonstrate very unpredictable behavior, as well as convulsions, an increased heart rate, and coma.

♣ Ecstasy- It is a drug produced often by underground chemists and is often available at parties, concerts and dance clubs. It is usually in the form of a powder, tablet or capsule and is swallowed or snorted. It is a hallucinogenic and a stimulant so that emotions become very intense. Users may experience tingly skin, depression, paranoia and a raised body temperature which can cause damage to organs.

The use of illegal drugs is increasing, especially among young teens. The average age of first marijuana use is fourteen, and alcohol use can start before age twelve. The use of marijuana and alcohol in high school has become common.

Drugs are chemicals that change how the body works, and your bloodstream carries them throughout the body, including to the brain. Depending on the drug, the amount taken, and other factors, drugs may deaden or intensify your senses, change your alertness, alter your perceptions, and lessen physical pain. They also shock your brain, heart and organs and can cause instant death and/or permanent damage. They are almost always psychologically and/or physically addictive, often from just a first time use.

Steroids have been in the news a lot lately with professional athletes. They are made from a derivative of the male sex hormone testosterone. They increase your body's ability to strengthen its muscles when working out, but they also cause a host of problems:

- Premature balding or hair loss.
- Dizziness.
- Mood swings, including anger, aggression, and depression.
- Believing things that aren't true (delusion).
- Extreme feelings of mistrust or fear (paranoia).
- Problems sleeping.
- Nausea and vomiting.
- Trembling.
- High blood pressure that can damage the heart or blood vessels over time.
- Aching joints.
- Greater chance of injuring muscles and tendons.
- Jaundice or yellowing of the skin; liver damage.
- Urinary problems.
- Shortening of final adult height.
- Increased risk of developing heart disease, stroke and some types of cancer.

Well, when I think of steroids I think of an image. You have the advantage over someone, which is a form of cheating. I guess it wouldn't be right unless it was legal for everybody. Reason it's not legal for everybody is because it can hurt people seriously.

– Evander Holyfield, Former World Heavyweight Boxing Champion

A lot of guys tell themselves they'll only use steroids for a season or a school year. Unfortunately, steroids can be addictive, making it hard to stop taking them. The consequences are so severe that professional sports leagues have banned them, but most steroid use in this country is during the high school years.

At some point, each of you will see—and have opportunity to use—alcohol and other drugs. Sadly, the use of alcohol and other drugs occurs among many middle and high school students around our country. It sometimes happens at the elementary school level. It happens to boys from all backgrounds.

What can you do to protect yourself from making poor and unwholesome decisions about drugs?

First of all, decide now about whether or not you will drink, smoke and use drugs. If you wait to make your decision until you are at a party and your best friend and the girl you like are handing you a beer, you will make the wrong decision. That's a guarantee. Make a decision when you can think about it from a very rational and long-term perspective. Think about it from the perspective of what God says on this subject. Know what you will say and do when confronted with the opportunity. Have more courage than to accept a beer, and then secretly pour it out or pretend to drink it. Rehearse what you will say. If you don't have the confidence simply to say "no way" and walk away, here are some other things you can say:

- ♣ "I'll get busted. My mom will smell it on breath. She said she is going to smell my breath and clothes when I come home."
- ♣ "My parents won't let me play on the basketball team if I drink or smoke, and they'll find out. Parents always eventually hear what happens at a party."
- ♣ "I don't get my driver's license if I drink or smoke. I'd rather drive as a junior and senior than drink a beer tonight."

♣ "I've got a goal not to drink this year, and I'm trying really hard to meet it. Help me, please."

♣ "My parents and I have a deal. They've promised me something awesome if I don't drink. I don't want to blow it."

Secondly, avoid putting yourself in situations where sin is likely to win out. The Bible tells us in Proverbs 1:15 not to set your foot on the paths of sinners who can entice you. So if you know that there will be drinking and drug use at a party, don't go. If you know that your buddy's parents are out of town and that their liquor cabinet is stocked, don't spend the night at his house. If you know a particular friend is very persuasive and is making poor choices, don't hang out with him on Friday nights. You will probably find that it's easier to say no in advance to attending an event than it is to say no to a beer or joint at the event itself.

Finally, know that drinking and using drugs don't make you a man. It's not a rite of passage or something you should do to "prove" you are older. It's not an adventure. Know that everyone these next few years is not doing it. Know that you're not invincible or immune from serious and deadly consequences (like many teenagers think they are). Know that, if you do these things, you will deeply disappoint those adults in your life who love you and have the wisdom to know what is best for your long-term growth into a man. More importantly, know that you will disappoint God.

Let's summarize. What is the big deal about alcohol and other drugs? Here is a short list:

♣ They damage your body, especially during adolescence when your body is really growing and developing. This damage can be permanent.

♣ They impair your judgment, and this leads to making a lot of other poor choices with serious, long-term consequences.

♣ They can kill you, sometimes from their chemical effects and sometimes from their broader effects (like drinking and driving). Some people die the first time they ever use a drug, even if it is a small quantity. Some people die from drinking too much alcohol.

♣ They stunt your personal, social and emotional development because your true self and your true feelings are hidden or suppressed.

- ♣ They damage your relationships, as they cause you either to lie to or disappoint many people who love you.

- ♣ They are addictive, meaning if you start using them, you may never be able to stop.

- ♣ They hinder your achievements: your performance, dedication and motivation suffer.

- ♣ You might be kicked off a team or club and removed from a leadership or prestigious positions.

- ♣ They are illegal, and you can go to jail if you use them. When you apply to college, graduate school, or for a job, you might automatically be disqualified from a school or position if you have a criminal record.

- ♣ Even more importantly, their illegal use and abuse are in defiance of God and short-circuit the great things He wants to provide us.

In spite of all of these dangers and downsides, why do teenagers drink, smoke and use other drugs? They do so because there is great peer pressure to do so. They do so because they are bored. They do so because they don't have healthy ways of dealing with their emotions. They do so because it can numb them to the doubts and disappointments they feel about themselves. We all have a hole deep inside of us, and we use a lot of things to try to fill it up, including alcohol and other drugs. The only thing that will ever fill that hole is knowing about—and accepting—the love and forgiveness of God through His son, Jesus. If you are sure of your value and worth from God, and if you will remind yourself of that, you are far less likely to feel the need to drink, smoke and use drugs.

Chapter 6
Questions for Reflection and Discussion

1. Have you already been in situations where there were opportunities for drinking, smoking and/or drug use? What did you do?

2. What are the differences between your parents having a beer or glass of wine and you drinking one?

3. Why do teenage boys drink, smoke and use other drugs?

4. What are the dangers of alcohol, tobacco and other drugs?

5. In what situations are you most likely to encounter alcohol, cigarettes and other drugs? Is it worth putting yourself in that situation?

6. What exactly will you say or do when someone hands you a beer?

7. What can you be doing to have wholesome adventures that can lessen your likelihood to pursue fake adventures with alcohol and other drugs?

8. When you feel lonely, disappointed or stressed, what do you do? Do you have a healthy way to address those feelings that will make you less likely to medicate them?

9. Have you asked your parents if you have any blood relatives who are alcoholics?

10. What man can you think of whose life has basically been ruined or cut short by alcohol, tobacco or other drugs?

11. If you are a Christian, are your decisions and actions about alcohol and other drugs helping or hurting your witness to other people?

Chapter 7

Girls Like Guys In Uniform

My boyfriend used to ask his mother, 'How can I find the right woman for me?' and she would answer, 'Don't worry about finding the right woman – concentrate on becoming the right man.'

– Girl, Age 21

I want my audience to know me for my work, not because of who I'm dating.

– Shia LeBeouf, Actor

Dating refers to an activity two people share together with the intention of getting to know each other better on a potentially romantic level.

Sometimes guys are preoccupied with the fact that they don't know what to say to a girl to show that they like her. Guys don't want to say "I like you. Will you go out with me?" because it sounds cheesy or they hear it doesn't work and it would be embarassing. They try to find some subtle way to show their admiration for that special girl. And finding that subtle way is what's difficult for guys. What a dilemma!

A guy and a girl can be just friends, but at one point or another, they will fall for each other...Maybe temporarily, maybe at the wrong time, maybe too late, or maybe forever.

– Dave Matthews Band

Over the next few years of your lives, you will become increasingly interested in and excited about girls. They will stir strong feelings in you—both positive and negative feelings. They will make you happy, excited and eager to be around them. They will make your heart flutter and your step quicken. And they will sometimes disappoint you and hurt your heart, especially when a girl lets you know she doesn't feel the same way about you that you might about her. Sometimes, they might simply confuse you. Teen relationships between boys and girls are often confusing, and even if you're not dating or have a girlfriend, it's easy to be confused about the fact you aren't in a relationship or dating or as into girls as some of your friends.

God built you to be attracted to girls and women. So the attraction that you feel—or will increasingly feel—is a wonderful and natural thing. At this point in your life, you may or may not be interested in girls, and that's fine. Some of you are more comfortable talking with and about girls than others are, and that's fine. There is no magical age or moment when you are suddenly supposed to be interested in girls. A lot of guys feel a pressure or expectation to have a girlfriend or date in middle school or high school. It causes a lot of anxiety. Like other things in our lives, an attraction to girls and a readiness to date unfolds at different times. Often, boys fake an interest in girls before they really feel an interest in them, and they begin dating and forming serious relationships before they are ready for them. There is not a thing wrong with not dating in middle school and high school. It doesn't mean you won't have girlfriends or get married later. It's often a sign of maturity.

A successful relationship of any sort takes work; just having a strong attraction and emotions, including the feeling of love, is not enough.

Relationships are based on serving one another:

- ♣ Putting her needs in front of your needs.
- ♣ Sacrificing what you may want.
- ♣ Doing special and unexpected things for her.

Don't be in a rush to be girl-crazy, to feel like you should be really interested in girls, or date or have a girlfriend.

Boy-girl relationships can be complicated—they can have painful and serious consequences, especially for the person who isn't ready for them.

So why is this so tough??

1.   Boy-girl relationships involve your self-esteem: what you think about yourself. We all want to feel good about ourselves, especially during the teenage years. Part of dating and relationships between boys and girls involves rejection—saying or sending messages like, "No, I don't want to date you," or "No, I don't like you," or "I think someone else is better than you," and so forth. It hurts deeply to be told that, especially when you really like the person. Your self-esteem can take a real beating, and you can damage the self-esteem of a girl.

2.   Boy-girl relationships often can make a person try to be someone he is not. We invent personalities for ourselves. We become actors—people we are not—in an effort to impress girls, to be the sort of person we think they want us to be and to be cool. It takes a lot of energy and thought to reinvent yourself; it's tiring and draining and disappointing to God who made us the way He did. Ultimately, it leads to confusion and doubts about yourself.

3.   Boy-girl relationships are potentially dangerous because they involve emotions, especially love. Teenage boys, no matter how smart they are, do not yet have the life experiences to fully understand love

and act out love for a girl. Teenagers, and even adults, often confuse crushes/ infatuation (an attraction based on superficial things) and lust (an attraction based on sexual desire) for love. It's like thinking that you can fly an airplane just because you have a driver's license for a car. You'll crash if you try to operate something too complicated (like love or an airplane) before you fully understand how it works. And a relationship crash can have very significant consequences.

4 Boy-girl relationships are potentially dangerous because they often involve making poor choices that are displeasing to God and which can have life-altering consequences. The changes in your bodies we will discuss in the next chapter produce strong urges sometimes to engage in sexual activities with girls. Additionally, much of our society—the movies, TV, many adults, some of your friends—will say that sexual activity outside of marriage is ok. The girl you really like, or that you think you love, may say it is ok also.

There are other reasons that boy-girl relationships during the teenage years can be potentially dangerous, but these are some important ones. So what do you do? Stay away from girls? No.

We think that one of the most important things you can do is to have a proper view of girls and relationships:

- Girls should be viewed as children of God created, like you, in His image.
- Girls should be treated with respect and kindness.
- Take your time getting to know girls.
- Get to know girls in a safe and comfortable environment before one-on-one dating. Go on group dates. Hanging out with a bunch of girls and guys is usually a safe and good way to spend time with girls.

One-on-one dating and having a girlfriend in middle school is neither necessary nor, usually, a good idea. Too many things can go wrong which can short-circuit the better experiences down the road. By the way, many boys in middle school who say they have a girlfriend have one in name only. They usually don't actually go out on dates, see each other, or even talk all that much. In middle school in particular, having a girlfriend is usually just for show, coolness and reputation.

Dating during the teen years, while exciting, can also be a little scary. Many teenagers want to begin dating, but they are uncomfortable with the idea of dating one-on-one. The best way to overcome this problem is to date in groups. This creates a low pressure environment where neither date has to do all the talking; their friends are there to help! Group dates are also a big hit with parents, who tend to let teenagers start dating earlier if they travel in packs.

Wait to date until you are ready to date for the right reasons. Wait until you have established standards for the sort of girl you want to date. Wait until you are mature enough to treat a girl as a sister in Christ. Wait until you are able to look at the inside of a girl as much as the outward appearance. Wait until you are mature enough not to need a girlfriend/date or have to brag about having one. Wait until you have committed yourself to not engaging in sexual activity outside of marriage. Wait until you are secure enough to withstand having your heart broken. In the meanwhile, enjoy them as friends, hang out in groups and get to know them.

Ever wish you could predict ahead of time whether or not a dating relationship will work out? It would save a lot of headaches and heartache, wouldn't it? While you can't predict the future, you can make choices that will help guide you to relationships that are both exciting and honoring to God. Here's how.

As you think through potential dates, ask yourself these questions:

- ♣ What's my first impression? "Don't judge a book by its cover." That's how the old saying goes. True, first impressions aren't totally accurate. But until you get to know a person, you must depend on first impressions. Who do they hang around with? What kind of parties do they go to? Do they drink, smoke, use drugs? This kind of "first impression" information is very helpful as you think about who you will or won't consider dating.

- ♣ How well do I know them? It always makes sense to go out with someone you've known for a while rather than a stranger.

- ♣ Do they treat others with respect? Ever been around a girl who can't do anything but put down her boyfriend? Ever spent time with a guy who likes to brag about how far he got on his last date? Not exactly the kind of people you want to trust with your self-image or your reputation.

♣ Do your values clash? Are the things most important to you also important to them? Are you headed in the same general direction in life? (For instance: you value good grades and plan to attend college; your potential date regularly cuts classes and has no plans for life after graduation.) Do they have decent standards when it comes to the movies and TV shows they watch? Are they committed, growing Christians who seek to live what they believe? You may be thinking, "But, hey, I've heard opposites attract!" Not a good dating rule to live by, especially when it comes to values, moral standards and personal beliefs.

♣ Do they keep their promises? If they've been in a serious dating relationship before, did they flirt with others or cheat on the person they were dating? It's good to keep in mind that a promise breaker can quickly become a heartbreaker, too.

When you are ready to date or have a girlfriend, here are some tips:

♣ Date and have a girlfriend for the right reasons. Don't do it to be cool or because other people are. Don't be pressured into dating because of expectations, including from your parents. A lot of guys don't date much or at all in high school, and that's fine. Often, guys who begin dating at a later age have better experiences with girls and girlfriends and healthier relationships because they have developed more maturity and self-assurance than they had at a younger age.

♣ Show extra-good manners around girls. As a sign of courtesy young men should:
　　♣ walk ahead of their date in a darkened theater or room.
　　♣ walk on the outside of the sidewalk, next to the road.
　　♣ stand when a girl the same age or a woman enters the room and stand when she leaves.
　　♣ wait until the women have been seated (and help them be seated if it is a formal date) before seating myself.
　　♣ don't start eating before your date.

- ♣ always thank a girl after a dance or date.

- ♣ opening car and building doors and is a sign of respect.

♣ Speak respectfully of all girls. If you develop a reputation for treating any girl poorly or saying inappropriate things about even one girl, we can almost assure you that many girls will hear about it, and this may hurt your chances of many girls wanting to be your friend or date you. The reputation you have among girls is important.

Girls definitely like it when a guy compliments them... as long as they are telling the truth. Don't feed her a bunch of lines... that's not cool. Also, do little things just to let her know that you are interested. Girls like to see that you would go out of your way to do little things

– Girl, Age 17

♣ Take the initiative and lead in the relationship. God charges men to take the initiative, and girls usually like that. Call them to talk or ask them out (Ask them out well in advance of the date night). Suggest the plans for what you will do on the date. Of course, make plans according to what you think she will like and be willing to change your plans, but take the responsibility to come up with the ideas.

♣ Take the lead in establishing the boundaries, intensity and pace of your relationship and talking about your relationship. That's your role, and don't neglect to do it, even if the girl is being more assertive and aggressive in pushing the relationship.

♣ Plan creative dates. Girls like it when they know you spent time thinking about them, and a creative date shows a lot of care. Girls especially like it when there are good opportunities for casual conversations on a date.

♣ Go slowly with your relationship. Good relationships are marathons, not sprints, and many relationships start out too quickly and intensely to last. You can't run a marathon at full speed. In the early stages of the relationship, resist the urge to talk every single day, to see each other at every opportunity, and to kiss and say "I love you" too soon. Your relationship will be much more likely to thrive and survive.

♣ Respect her future. Remember that you are with someone's future wife. You do not want to do anything that would damage her future relationships. You would not want a guy doing something inappropriate with your sister. Keep that in mind as you are dating.

We have loaded you with information about girls, dating and relationships but we know you really want to read about one subject: kissing. Kissing is a great thing. It feels really good. It's exciting (and nerve-racking at first). You should understand, though, that kissing is meant to lead to sex. God designed it as foreplay to sex; it wasn't meant to be a stopping point. Once you start kissing, it can lead you and the girl down a slippery slope toward sex. So you need to show discipline and restraint in how you kiss, where you kiss, and how long you kiss. To keep from sliding down the slippery slope to sex, we suggest short kisses—a few seconds—and kisses on the cheek or with the mouth closed. Long kisses and open-mouth kisses fire up your sexual engines, making you want to touch more of a girl's body. Kisses on a sofa, or in seclusion from anyone else, are also more dangerous than a kiss at the front door.

If you kiss on the first date and it's not right, then there will be no second date. Sometimes it's better to hold out and not kiss for a long time. I am a strong believer in kissing being very intimate, and the minute you kiss, the floodgates open for everything else.

– Jennifer Lopez, Actress

Save your first kiss. Don't give your first kiss away quickly or cheaply, and know that kissing can mess things up. All of a sudden, when you kiss a girl, it signifies you are more than friends. You and/or she may not be ready for that. It introduces new pressures, expectations and roles. It may make things awkward. A lot of good friendships get short-circuited by a kiss too soon. Kissing is personal and private and most appropriately done when someone is actually your girlfriend. Wait on kissing for a while.

The worst thing a man can ever do is kiss me on the first date.

– Halle Berry, Actress

Do you ask a girl if you can kiss her before you actually kiss her? That can certainly be a good idea, though it may change the surprise and mood of the moment. You will probably not have to ask her, but you should have a good sense for this based on your relationship. If the two of you know each other very well and have gone out on several dates, then you will know. A kiss on the cheek is always a more appropriate first kiss than one on the lips.

The first kiss I had was the most disgusting thing in my life. The girl injected about a pound of saliva into my mouth, and when I walked away I had to spit it all out.

– Leonardo DiCaprio, Actor

Before you kiss a girl, though, you need to think through some questions. The most important question is to figure out what you are trying to communicate to her with a kiss. Are you simply trying to communicate to her that you really like her, or are you trying to communicate to her that you want to touch her? There is a big difference between affection and lust. Know your true motives. You also need to think through the status of your relationship with her. Will kissing mess up something good? Are you ready for new pressures? Is she ready for them? Is she special enough to you that she is worthy of your kiss?

But how do you know if you really like this girl or even love her? Guys your age and some men struggle with knowing the difference between infatuation, lust and love. So what's the difference?

Infatuation is often short-lived and often based on superficial things when you don't really know a girl very well. An infatuation is like when a new video game comes out; it's really cool and new for a while, but then you lose interest in it and want something newer and different. You may go through several infatuations in the next few years.

Lust is an attraction based only on physical attributes and stirring up physical desires and responses in you. Guard yourself against lust.

Love, on the other hand, is a deep, complex and mature emotion and set of actions.

When do I know I love someone? When do I tell her I love her? Both are very difficult questions to answer, especially at your age. Don't say "I love you" until you know what it means and how it will change your relationship. Remember that love is not just a feeling. Those three words mean sacrifice and service, commitment and protection. Those three words change the expectations of the relationship; they bring pressure. They up the stakes and intensity of the relationship. Serious relationships often bring teenagers a lot of stress, tears and agony because they are not yet equipped emotionally to handle the pressures and demands of a serious relationship.

Ask yourself this question on a regular basis: do I love her, do I love it that she loves me, or do I love being in love? Those are three very different things. The last two are not love. While they may feel good, they are shallow and selfish and signs you are not ready for love or have a mature enough understanding of it to be saying you love a girl. Try to figure out what's really going on with your heart and head.

As we end this chapter, we want to give you some practical advice on how to navigate dating and relationships in a way that is healthy and glorifying to God:

1 Don't put yourself in tempting situations in which you can make bad decisions about alcohol, drugs and sex. We'll discuss sex in the next chapter, but the temptations during the teenage years can sometimes be too great, so it's wise to decide in advance to avoid a place or situation in which you could make a poor choice.

2 Make sure you are maintaining a proper balance in your life. Girlfriends can easily create an imbalance in your life. It's easy to invest too much of your time, emotions and energy in a girl. Even if your grades, activities and other relationships are slipping, you will likely have a blind-spot to this, so ask your parents and friends if they see an imbalance that needs to be corrected. Also, be careful not to damage your friendships with your buddies by neglecting them as you spend too much time with your girlfriend.

3 Respect your parents' rules and boundaries, and listen to them. We'll talk about parents a lot in a later chapter, but for now, know that they have more wisdom on relationships than you do, and any rules and boundaries they may be imposing regarding a girl or relationship are probably wise ones that will benefit you. So, respect it and them, and we suggest that you seek their advice about girls. Also, practice treating your mom the way you would a date. Hold doors for her like you would a date.

4 Go out of your way to gain the respect of your date's parents. Get to know them. Be honest with them. Don't put up on an act just so they will like you. Ask them if you can take their daughter out on a date. This sounds old-fashioned, but it's critical. A girl's parents can practically make or break you. They will probably assume that how you treat them will be how you treat their daughter. They will also have a big influence on how their daughter thinks about you.

5 Learn about the needs and preferences of girls. As you get older, you'll realize that men and women have some important differences. If you try to relate to girls the way you do to boys, you'll have a difficult time with your relationships. Know that most girls will feel a connection to you if you communicate well with them rather than simply share an activity. She wants you to share your emotions. She probably wants you to listen rather than solve her problem. She may feel your affection more clearly when you wash her car or give her your undivided attention than when you rent a fancy limo for the prom. Don't assume that the way you like to feel affection and affirmation is the same way she does.

What (most) Christian girls wish guys knew:

1 Listening is better than fixing. When a girl feels emotional or has a problem and turns to a guy friend to talk about it, she may not be ready to fix it. She just wants to talk about it and feel like the guy understands.

2 Friendship really matters. Some girls get frustrated because lots of guys don't seem to be interested in friendship if there's not a shot at something more.

3 Real Christian men respect women. Christian guys sometimes get the idea that it's okay to talk badly about girls when they're not around—to make comments about their bodies, to mock them for their moods, to treat them unkindly simply because they're women. That is always, always wrong.

4 Looks do matter, but not as much as what's inside. Girls want to be with men they can respect for their strength, integrity and commitment.

5 "Put me second." They're looking for a guy who has made God number one in his life above everything, including them.

6 Break up respectfully. It is unlikely that you will marry anyone you date as a teenager, so anyone you are in a relationship with will involve a breakup. Breakups usually involve a lot of pain for at least one person, so it should be done with care and compassion and in person—never by email, a text message or through someone else—and with respect for her reputation. Also, the manner and care of the breakup will probably be known to all of her friends, and you would regret damage to your reputation if you are thoughtless and insensitive. Remember as well, and very importantly, you are dating someone else's future wife, so you should respect her and her future husband by how you treat, protect and break up with her.

7 Date other believers. The Bible instructs Christians to marry fellow believers. A fellow believer can—and should—encourage your walk with the Lord. A romantic relationship with someone with a different set of beliefs can be like juggling dynamite.

Developing meaningful relationships with girls is a great adventure. There will be ups and downs, but holding a Biblical perspective on girls and relationships can even out the bumps of the next few years.

Chapter 7
Questions for Reflection and Discussion

1. Do you have feelings of attraction for girls yet? If so, is it an infatuation, lust or love?

2. What does God say about how we are to think about girls? When you think about girls, what goes through your mind?

3. What are the right reasons to date and be in a relationship with a girl? Do you want to date or have a girlfriend because it's a cool thing to do?

4. What are the characteristics of a girl you want to date?

5. What potential dangers could girls bring me?

6. Are you secure enough to be rejected and have your heart broken by a girl?

7. What are some of your responsibilities as the male on a date or in a relationship?

8. What are the keys to a successful male/female relationship?

9. What is love?

10. Do you think teenage boys are equipped to handle serious relationships with girls? Why or why not?

11. Why is it important to date someone of a similar faith to you?

Chapter 8

Afterburners On!

Puberty was very vague. I literally locked myself in a room and played guitar.

— Johnny Depp, Actor

Becoming a man means your body is going to start changing, but do not be alarmed or think it is only happening to you, because it is happening to your friends too.

— Thomas, Age 14

Fighter pilots fly high performance jet planes in combat. Their primary job is to defend our troops and positions against attacks by enemy aircraft.

To become a fighter pilot, you first must join the Air Force or the Navy as they are the ones in the U.S. who utilize fighter planes. The Marines have some attack aircraft, but mostly fly support for Marines on the ground. The Army uses mostly helicopters, while the Coast Guard uses aircraft for rescue. Neither the Army nor the Coast Guard engage in extensive air to air combat. For Americans, the only domestic employers of fighter pilots are the U.S. Air Force, the Marines and the U.S. Navy.

All pilots in both the United States Air Force and Navy are commissioned officers, and all commissioned officers in these two branches must be college graduates. So the first requirement for a fighter pilot is to be a college graduate. The next requirement is that you meet the physical, psychological and intellectual requirements for admission to officer training. The next few years of your life will be a physical and psychological test for you. The information in this chapter is critical in helping you go through the next stage of your life.

Around your age, you are beginning the adventuresome yet potentially dangerous transition from being a boy to becoming a man. You are leaving your boyhood behind. Many things will soon begin to change, if they have not already. Perhaps the most noticeable change will be your body. Around the same time your body starts to change, you will become more aware of girls as well. Eventually, you will see how these changes in your body and your awareness and interest in girls will fit together one day as part of God's great plan for you as a man. For now, let's start by looking at this time in your life when your body undergoes its most significant transformation since you were a little baby. This phase of life is often called puberty.

What is puberty?

Puberty is a time in each person's life when his body starts changing from a child body to an adult body. It's a time of often rapid and intense physical changes. It is a sometimes confusing, sometimes uncomfortable process, even for those people who seem so secure and happy on the outside. The biological changes not only impact your body, including your ability to have sex and your desire for it, but they will have an impact on your thoughts and emotions as well. Every boy should know what to expect in the upcoming years, why it is happening, and how it is a part of God's plan. Knowing this, especially knowing how normal and natural this is, can reduce your anxieties, discomforts and insecurities in the upcoming years. Let's look at what actually happens during puberty.

Questions Boys Are Asking About Puberty:

- ♣ When will I get muscles?
- ♣ What's up with body hair?
- ♣ Do I think about girls too much or not enough?
- ♣ Why do I smell?

What happens?

One day, around your age now, your pituitary gland in your brain will send a message to your testicles to start making a hormone called testosterone. A hormone is a chemical. This testosterone chemical will go from your testicles where it is made and travel, via your blood, throughout your whole body. If you were a girl, your body would make two different chemicals (estrogen and progesterone) in your ovaries instead of testicles.

Anyway, this testosterone that starts running through your body does a few things:

- Your voice gets deeper.

- You grow to pretty much your full height. As you grow, you may be somewhat clumsier than you are now until you get used to your new size. And your joints will sometimes ache as your body grows.

- Your skin becomes oilier, causing pimples and acne. Sometimes, no matter how many times you wash your face with Neutrogena or how much Clearasil cream you put on or how many times you see the dermatologist, you will have some acne.

- You start to grow hair under your arm and on your face, starting with the mustache area, chin and sideburns. This is usually somewhat later. By the way, don't be in a rush to shave. It's a pain.

- Your sweat glands begin working and you sweat more. Once you hit puberty, you definitely don't want to be without deodorant, especially around a girl. It would probably be a good idea to start using deodorant now if you aren't yet.

- Your muscles and strength increase.

- Your penis and testicles get bigger.

- You develop pubic hair around your groin and testicles. The hair helps keep the testicles warm enough to produce sperm. (We're about to get to that.)

- Your testicles start to make semen and produce millions of sperm. Semen is a fluid, which contains sperm, which is what enables you to produce a child with a woman.

- You have the ability to ejaculate, which is when your erect penis shoots out semen and its sperm.

- You will begin having frequent and strong sexual feelings, including sometimes when you least expect or want to. This will sometimes involve having erections at both expected and unexpected times, occasionally having wet dreams at night and feeling the urge to masturbate (We'll talk about wet dreams and masturbation later in this chapter).

Don't be ashamed or embarrassed by this. It's God's handiwork. It's the way he designed us to go from being a boy to becoming a man. Let's take a look at what God is up to with puberty. Here are, we think, God's three key purposes for puberty:

- ♣ God wants us to grow into men, with grown-up capabilities.
- ♣ Puberty is necessary for us to have the children God may bless us with.
- ♣ God wants us to lead a joyful and pleasurable life.

Those are all great things. We are so thankful that boys turn into men. Life is much fuller and more rewarding as men than as boys. Be grateful that God is going to turn you into a man.

I made you grow like a plant of the field. You grew up and developed and became the most beautiful of jewels. Your breasts were formed and your hair grew, you who were naked and bare.

– Ezekiel 16:7

Note in this passage that it is God that is doing this. The verse begins with I, referring to God. It is not something we humans control. You may have probably already begun puberty; perhaps it will start in the next few months, or you may begin it in a year or so from now. You are not worthy of any more or less respect based on when you begin puberty. There are no long-term consequences to when you begin it. So just relax and know that it will happen to you exactly when God wants it to. One other thing: puberty is not something to be laughed at because you are making fun of God's handiwork and God Himself since we were all created in His image. Just as importantly, you are not to make fun of anyone for his or her stage of puberty, whether they are entering it a bit earlier or a bit later.

Sex researchers have long known that teenagers often compromise their moral standards because not to do so would put their popularity at risk.

– Tony Campolo, Author, "Growing up in America"

How does puberty relate to sex, and what exactly is sex?

A lot of puberty relates to sex. Sex is not a dirty word. It should not be a mysterious word. God, in fact, created sex for us to enjoy, but there are a lot of lies about sex and a great deal of misinformation. If most or all that you know about sex comes from TV, movies or the Internet, then you will have a stunted and narrow view of sex and women, and you are at great risk for making many poor, unwholesome and unhealthy choices. If most or all that you know about sex comes from your friends or an older sibling, then you probably don't have all the facts and a mature perspective on the topic.

It is important that you understand the biology of sex. It is even more important that you have a Biblical understanding of sex. Let's see what God has to say about sex. He has a lot to say about it. One entire book of the Bible, Song of Solomon, centers on the courtship, engagement, wedding, marriage and sexual attraction and fulfillment that a man and woman share. The book talks about his longing for her, the beauty of her body, and even their sex on their wedding night. We as men are made to see the beauty of women and feel passion and longing for them. We are made even to crave to be intimate with them, to want to have sex with them.

As this entire book of the Bible illustrates, sex is a beautiful act God created for a husband and wife to enjoy. Many married couples often have sex 1-2 times a week because it is so special and powerful. It is an act of passion, intimacy, joy and procreation.

When a husband and wife have sex, it is a very deep, most intimate act, exposing one's emotions, vulnerabilities and hopes. It involves the whole being—not just a body part. It is a spiritual act of marriage, created and blessed by God to bring us closer to our spouse. It's a lot more than a physical, biological act, but let's start with just its physical nature.

Sexual intercourse is the main act of sex. The Bible describes sexual intercourse as when two fleshes become one flesh (Genesis 2:24). It starts when the man inserts his penis, which is erect or hard, into the woman's vagina. It is erect or hard because he is sexually aroused by the woman. The vagina is a small opening—maybe an inch—in the groin area of a woman. For several minutes, the penis will rub or stroke back and forth inside the vagina. This is very pleasurable physically for both the man and the woman, because on the end of the penis and around the woman's vagina are millions of nerve cells which are very sensitive to any sort of touch. After several minutes of this intense pleasure, which is getting stronger and stronger and stronger with all of these nerve cells being stimulated, the man will ejaculate (this is an orgasm). During this ejaculation, semen will shoot out his penis up into the woman's vagina. The semen contains millions of sperm—your genes, your genetic makeup—which if the conditions are right and it reaches an egg inside the woman, a baby will be created. The semen that the man ejaculates into the woman—enough to fill a couple of spoonfuls in all—looks like a mixture of milk and mayonnaise.

Before puberty, your testicles do not produce the semen and sperm necessary to conceive a child with a woman. Now, at puberty, you are physically and biologically able to father a child. Additionally, the testosterone, which is now racing through your body, will begin to stir urges to do this very thing. You will out of nowhere experience these sexual urges and thoughts you have never felt before. It might be when you see a certain girl or think about a certain woman you saw in a movie; it may be in the middle of math class or in the middle of the night or when you wake up in the morning. As the testosterone stirs these sexual impulses, blood rushes to the tissue in the penis, making it hard. Starting in puberty, this may happen 7-10 times a day, or more, as testosterone has 7-10 or more big spurts through the body each day. Don't panic when this happens. It's normal. Remember, God made each of us the way we are, with testosterone surging through our bodies during adolescence. In Genesis 1:31, God said He was very pleased with what He made. And God created everything.

Depending on your age, it may seem foreign to you that sex would be appealing. Just thinking about the act of sex seems gross to children. Probably the idea of being naked in front of a girl seems impossible and utterly embarrassing. Over the next few years, you will think about sex differently than you do right now. Your mind will start to understand that it can be something that men and women find great pleasure in.

Now that you know that God created sex as a joyful, pleasurable and intimate act, let's see if He puts any restrictions on it. God actually does place restrictions on it, not to keep us from enjoying life, but to protect us and to enable us to grow into the sort of men that He envisions for us. His restrictions are acts of love, like parents who tell their children not to play in the street or with a loaded gun. Let's look at them.

Florida quarterback Tim Tebow is a virgin. At the 2009 SEC Media Days, a reporter asked Tim Tebow if he is a virgin, to which Tim replied, "Yes, I am." First,

I'm not sure what that question had to do with college football and the Florida Gators. And second, that's a pretty bold question to ask anyone, let alone a super star athlete. But was anyone surprised by his answer? Tim has never strayed from his faith and is as openly Christian as anyone we've ever seen. Part of the Christian faith is to save yourself for marriage… to not engage in premarital sex. Tim follows the Bible, so it's no surprise that he follows this part of the scripture as well.

The most important restriction on sex is that God wants you only to have sex in marriage with your wife. No sex before you are married. He doesn't say, "If you are in love, you may have sex," or "If you have a serious girlfriend, you may have sex," or "If it's a special occasion with a girl, you may have sex." He doesn't say, "Once you are an adult, you may have sex." He says that sex is only blessed in marriage. And once you are married, you may not have sex with anyone who is not your wife. The Bible is very clear about this. The term for anyone who has sex with someone other than his or her spouse is an "adulterer." Let's see what the Bible says about sex and adultery.

Hebrews 13:4 makes this pretty clear. "Marriage should be honored by all, and the marriage bed kept pure, for God will judge the adulterer and all the sexually immoral." Genesis recounts the experience of Jacob, who loves Rachel, but he waits to have sex with her until he is allowed to marry her. Look at what Jacob says to her father in Genesis 29:21. "Then Jacob said to Laban, 'Give me my wife. My time is completed, and I want to lie with her.'" Notice the order: marriage and then sex. He was obviously very attracted to her. He loved her. But he knew he was supposed to marry her before having sex.

Genesis also has another story that illustrates that God forbids sex outside of marriage. Joseph, as a young man, was working for a man named Potipher, and Potipher's wife, probably a beautiful woman, attempted to seduce Joseph. She invites him to have sex with her. What does Joseph do? He flees from the room. Joseph knows he should not have sex with a woman who is not his wife.

So what are the Bible's key messages about sex? Here they are:

✦ Sex is a gift from God for married couples, and it is only blessed in marriage. We must avoid sex outside of marriage (Hebrews 13:4; Jacob and Rachel in Genesis 29:21; Joseph and Potiphar's wife in Genesis 39:9)

✦ Sex is an act of unity (Genesis 2:24; I Corinthians 6:15-18)

- ♣ Our bodies are temples for the Holy Spirit, and we are to honor God with our bodies (I Corinthians 6:19)

- ♣ We will be judged by God for sex outside of marriage (Hebrews 13:4)

- ♣ We are to avoid sexual immorality and control our bodies (I Thessalonians 4:3)

Sex is a powerful act, able both to create life and to destroy or derail a life. It's like a fire. If you deliberately and carefully build a fire in a brick fireplace in your home, it adds warmth, comfort, light, beauty and enjoyment. If you build the same fire in the middle of your living room (not in a fireplace), it will burn your whole house down. Only when you place sex in marriage, like a fire in a fireplace, does the true blessing of its intended purpose take place.

Sex is not just a physical thing. It involves emotions – emotions that are hard to overcome once you break up. You feel as if he used you if you break up.

– Beth, Age 16

The following is a story from a college senior looking back to mistakes he has made:

"I first had intercourse with my girlfriend when we were 15. I'd been going with her for almost a year, and I loved her very much. She was friendly, outgoing, charismatic. We'd done everything but have intercourse, and then one night she asked if we could go all the way.

A few days later, we broke up. It was the most painful time of my life. I had opened myself up to her more than I had to anybody, even my parents.

I was depressed, moody, nervous. My friends dropped me because I was so bummed out. I felt like a failure. I dropped out of sports. My grades weren't terrific.

I didn't go out again until I got to college. I've had mostly one-night stands in the last couple of years. I'm afraid of falling in love."

If you break up with a guy you didn't have sex with, so what? You can walk away free. But if you break up with a guy you did have sex with, it stays on your mind. You worry over it in a haunting way.

– Jackie, Age 15

What happens to you when you have sex outside of marriage? There are a lot of problems, some of which may be immediate, while others are more long-term. It is a fire that burns and scars you and others. Here are some of the problems:

- It hurts your relationship with God by disobeying Him. Our disobedience of God grieves Him, and it can cause you to distance yourself from Him.

- You will emotionally hurt or damage yourself. You will feel guilt, shame, worry, dirty, confused and so forth. You will, if not at first then before too long, like yourself a whole lot less. God says to love ourselves.

- You will damage your relationship with the girl with whom you have sex. It's impossible to have a normal and healthy relationship with a girl if you have had sex with her. Some people think having sex brings two people closer together. If they are married it does; if they are not married, it will make things so awkward and confusing that it will drive them apart.

- You will emotionally hurt or damage a girl. She will, almost immediately and then increasing over time, feel guilty, used, cheap and betrayed by you. Her self-esteem will be damaged because of what you did with her. God says to love our neighbors as ourselves. As men, we are to protect, nurture, cherish and serve the girls and women in our lives.

- You will lose respect in the eyes of your peers—boys and girls. You will quickly get a bad reputation, which may take years to overcome. Girls will be less likely to want to be your friend, and that special girl you may want to date may also be far less likely to want to go out with you.

- You will have a harder time figuring out what love is. What is love? It is to nourish and cherish as you would your own body. It protects and provides at all times. Read I Corinthians 13:4-13. "Love is patient, kind, does not envy, does not boast, is not proud; it is not rude or self-seeking;

it is not easily angered; it keeps no record of right and wrongs. It protects, always trusts, always hopes, always perseveres." Love is very demanding and complicated and involves more maturity and experiences than teenagers have. Premarital sex confuses the complicated emotion of love. More than that, it violates what love is. Premarital sex is the very opposite of love. It is impatient and selfish. It does not preserve her sexual purity or yours.

♣ You will disappoint the woman you marry one day because you did not save yourself for her. On your wedding night, it is an incredible gift that you can give your wife if you can tell her that you have saved your sexual purity all of these years for her. You will be blown away by the power of the same gift from her. Exchanging these gifts on your wedding night can be an awesome and a tremendous way to start your marriage in a very strong way. On the other hand, if you have sex with a girl who does not turn out to be your wife, you are taking what doesn't belong to you. Her sexual purity and integrity belongs to her future husband. Don't rob him and her of that gift.

♣ You may get sexually transmitted diseases (STDs), some of which can last a lifetime or kill you.

♣ You may become a father before you are ready, and this will alter the course of your life forever. It is difficult and extremely demanding to be a father as an adult. To do it well takes a maturity, set of worldly experiences, and a large investment of time and energy that teenagers simply do not have. To be a teenage father will mean that you will likely shortchange three lives: your own, your child's, and the mother's. All three of you deserve better than that.

Wait until you're married. Most guys out there are users and you'll end up getting hurt, having a bad reputation, and more than likely, in the long run, being alone.

– Anonymous, Age 17

Those are some of the reasons why He says to wait on sex until you are married. God loves you and doesn't want these things to happen to you. He loves you and wants what is best for you (Jeremiah 29:11). He wants to protect and provide for you. He knows what pleasure it will bring you in marriage and what problems it will bring you outside of marriage.

Despite these warnings, dangers and damage, many teenage boys have sex anyway. They often do so because they believe the lies about sex. They think it is a rite of passage to becoming a man. They think or hear, "You aren't really a man until you have sex with a girl. You will feel more like a man when you have had sex." That's a lie. Real men protect. They protect girls from the damage that sex will have on them. Real men nurture and serve the girls and women in their lives. They don't let their selfish desires and lusts rule the day. They control their bodies.

Satan can easily seduce you with a whole lot of other lies as well. He may whisper that it will provide you with fulfillment and wholeness, which we all want and need. He may tell you that it will bring you and your girlfriend closer together, that you are old enough for sex, that it's ok if you love her, and that the Bible's notions on sex are simply outdated. You may think that you have the emotional maturity to handle a sexual relationship. You may think it is ok because it seems that so many people are doing it.

These are all lies, and they are very seductive and sophisticated ones. Beware. And beware of where you get your values and standards. Almost every prime-time TV show and movie today has at least one sex scene or various references to sex, and most of those involve an unmarried couple. Sex does seem to be everywhere. It seems to be casual. It seems to be all right if it brings both individuals pleasure. You must make a choice. Your decision about sex is ultimately a decision of whom you follow. Do you follow God or the pleasures and people of a sinful world? What will have more influence on you: the Holy Bible or Hollywood?

Beware also of a few other things that can trip you up in the difficult challenge to remain sexually pure until your wedding night. Here are a few of those things:

- ⚘ Pornography—because you come to view women as sex objects as opposed to children of God.
- ⚘ Alcohol and Drugs—because they cloud your judgment and remove the naturally healthy inhibitions we have that keep us from sex outside marriage.

- Not reading the Scriptures—you forget that God commands us very clearly not to have sex outside of marriage.

- The need to be cool—people will respect me for having had sex (when, in actuality, they and you will do just the opposite).

- Not deciding now whether or not you will wait until marriage to have sex—because the passions and physical excitement of the moment gather such momentum that you and the girl cannot stop short of sex. If you wait to make the decision on sex until you and a girl are in the backseat of your car or on the sofa when no one is home, you will have sex with her.

- Putting yourself in a situation where it's too easy to have sex.

This sex stuff probably seems a long way away. It will be here before you know it. But there are two other things related to puberty and sex that give teenage boys a lot of confusion and embarrassment: wet dreams and masturbation. We think it's better to go ahead and give you some perspective on them now.

You will have nocturnal emissions, more commonly called wet dreams. This happens when you release semen while you are sleeping. You will wake up and notice that your underpants are a little wet and sticky. The biological sexual pressures that have been building are released in the form of a wet dream. Don't panic, worry or be embarrassed when this happens on occasion. No one but you will probably know this happened.

You will probably feel the urge to masturbate. Masturbation is when you stimulate your penis for several minutes by rubbing and touching it until you have an orgasm (semen comes out the penis as it does during sex or during a wet dream). During the teenage years, you may fairly frequently feel the urge to masturbate. Occasional masturbation is typical of most teenage boys. People have different thoughts on the topic of masturbation. In his book, *Preparing For Adolescence*, Dr. James Dobson describes the guilt that many boys have when they fear that God can't love them because they masturbate. Dr. Dobson's father took his son aside in early adolescence and told him that he struggled with guilt over this as a boy, and that, though he hopes his son wouldn't do it, he should not to worry too much about it and not let it destroy his faith in God. Dr. Dobson writes that this type of compassion and reasonable faith helped him not to feel he needed to rebel against his parents or God.

We tend to agree with Dr. Dobson's perspective on masturbation. If the temptation should overcome you and you do it on occasion, don't be so consumed by guilt and shame that it interferes with your understanding of God's love for you, and don't let it cause you to take on absurd and unhealthy worries. Some teenage boys worry that masturbation may cause bodily damage or hinder their ability to have sex or children one day. It doesn't. Some teenage boys worry that doing it means they are a pervert or gay. It doesn't. A teenage boy may worry that he is the only person who does this. He isn't. Some teenage boys worry that doing this means they are going to hell and that God doesn't love them. That isn't right, either.

The urge to masturbate is natural for teenage boys, and the temptation is common, yet God calls us to live holy lives. Paul reminds us that the body is always a poor master but can be a useful slave. In other words, don't let your bodily urges control you, but instead control and use your body in ways that please God.

If you do masturbate, think about a few questions:

♣ What is your motivation for masturbating? Knowing that God designed you to glorify Him in everything you do, you should consider your reasons. If your reason for doing it is more than the occasional release of the sexual pressures that your teenage body has naturally built up, then you should especially examine your motivation. Similarly, if you are masturbating with great frequency, then you should pause and consider what is going on in your life.

♣ Is pornography fueling this and causing you the great frequency and perhaps addiction to masturbation? Pornography can do that. Perhaps a reason for excessive masturbation is that it produces a momentary fantasy or pleasure that covers an emptiness or loneliness you are feeling in life. If that is the case, you need to consider how you can fill that emptiness in your heart. The only true and complete way to do this is through understanding and accepting the love and forgiveness God offers you though Jesus Christ.

Another important topic to cover is oral sex. Mouth to sexual organ contact is often referred to as oral sex. Some teenagers, including some Christian ones, may tell you that oral sex is ok because it is not sexual intercourse. We disagree very strongly. Oral sex is sex. It is an act of sex, as is the touching, rubbing, kissing or sucking of the sexual organs. God's prohibition against sex outside of marriage includes all sexual acts, not simply the act of intercourse.

What about homosexuality, as in a sexual relationship between two men? It's a sensitive and scary topic, but it's a real one. In recent years, there has been more open talk about homosexuality, and it's been the subject of some mainstream television shows and movies. But just because it's a bit more in the mainstream culture doesn't mean God's instruction about it has changed; it's not simply a different but acceptable lifestyle choice. As with all the topics in this book, we are most interested in what God says about it. He's very clear. A sexual relationship between two men is a sin. Leviticus 18:22 says, "Do not lie with a man as one lies with a woman; that is detestable." At other places in both the Old and New Testaments, cities are condemned for various practices, including homosexuality. God tells us back in Genesis how he designed us— for a man and woman to be one flesh. Sex between two men goes against His creation and design.

Some boys worry that they may be gay if they glance at a naked friend or man in the locker room, or if they wonder how physically developed a classmate is. Most guys, though they would never admit it, have that curiosity and take some glimpses. Don't sweat that. Also, if you don't feel a strong attraction to girls yet, and if you don't feel like dating as a teenager, that also doesn't mean you're gay. Nor does it mean you're gay if you dress in a certain way or have certain interests.

While a sexual relationship between two men is sinful, sometimes Christians condemn homosexuality so loudly that they seem to forget about a whole lot of other sins that God tells us about and to avoid. Some men are tempted most strongly by greed; others by money; others may be tempted more strongly to lust after another woman and to have sex outside of marriage. For all of us, no matter what specific temptations are strongest, we are to restrain ourselves from falling to all of these temptations, including a sexual relationship with another man, and we are to treat all of our fellow sinners with compassion. If you are struggling with questions about your sexual preference, pursue someone to talk to.

For all of the sexual issues in this chapter, the most important thing you need to do is to understand the Biblical perspective on sex and make a commitment to remain sexually pure until you are married. There will be temptations along the way. God will give you the strength to overcome them. There will be awkward moments along the way with your body. Know that they are normal. You will feel sexual urges. Don't pollute your mind with pornography and the like, and they will more easily and quickly pass. Finally, think of girls not in sexual terms, but as friends to get to know and enjoy on your path to manhood.

While most of what we have covered in this chapter has been about the body and sex, puberty and adolescence also have an impact on your emotions, and especially the anger you may sometimes express or feel. With all the pressures of the teenage years and with all the testosterone surging through your body in new and unpredictable ways, it can definitely predispose you to be more volatile and angrier than you were as a child, so you need to be aware of this, understand anger and figure out an appropriate way to deal with it.

Anger is what psychologists call a secondary emotion, meaning that the real or primary feeling is some other emotion, usually fear or frustration that then gets expressed in an angry outburst. Many teenage boys get frustrated because they are yearning for independence from their parents and resent guidance from them, yet get they still need some of it. This creates a tension or frustration that the teenage boy may feel but not quite understand, and the frustration gets expressed as anger. At the same time, the teenage years are full of fears: things like not being popular or being picked on or not being smart enough. These fears show up as angry outbursts, sometimes at people or in situations that are unconnected. Parents are the unfair target of many tantrums.

Besides frustration and fear, the other main emotions that often are expressed as anger are embarrassment and inadequacy. If your mom treats you like a child in front of your friends, or your dad is listening to weird music while he's driving you and your friends to the movies, you may be embarrassed, but you are more likely to lash out at them angrily later rather than tell them they embarrassed you. Making a bad grade, feeling unsure around girls, not being selected for the music group—all of these things can make you feel inadequate, once again producing an emotion of anger. A sense of loss also can lead to anger, and there are a lot of losses during adolescence: the security of childhood, certain friendships, a predictable body, and sometimes the marriage of your parents. The adolescent years are full of things that can produce angry outbursts, and, at the same time, the body is full of testosterone to further fuel it.

It is very valuable to understand what is really happening when you are angry. It can help you to mange you anger in ways that are more appropriate and healthy. Similarly, it is crucial for you to learn to talk about your emotions rather than waiting until something explodes later. For the boy or man who doesn't learn to talk about his emotions and what is really on his heart, his most common and comfortable way to express most emotions may be anger, even if he is really feeling hurt or loneliness or some other feeling that should naturally be expressed in a different way.

When you are angry, though, it is usually a good idea to take a time-out before you say or do something that will make things worse. Many of the worst decisions a person can make are when he's mad. Go exercise or write in a journal. Listen to some music. Walk away from a fight. Pray. Prayer, especially prayer for someone who's made you upset, has a way of softening your heart and melting anger. Then, when you've calmed down, go deal with it in a constructive and honest way. And if you need to apologize to a parent, sibling or friend, do so. You'll feel better.

Between the body and the emotions, puberty causes a lot of tough situations to deal with. It's a time, more than ever before, when knowing of God's love for you—and His design and plans for you—can make a huge difference. When the big picture makes sense, and when you know how it turns out, it's a lot easier to find your way, to smooth out the bumps in the road and to enjoy the journey. Remember that God designed you carefully, that He has a plan for men and that He has a plan for you as a fully developed man.

Chapter 8
Questions for Reflection and Discussion

1. What is God's purpose and plan for sex?

2. How does puberty relate to sex?

3. Think about the movies and TV shows you watch and the music you listen to. What messages about sex does it send? How do those messages compare to God's message in the Bible?

4. If an unmarried couple is in love and has been dating for a long time, what is wrong with having sex?

5. What are the dangers and downside of sex?

6. What physical acts with a girl to whom I am not married are pleasing to God?

7. What do you think the situation would be in which you would be most likely to have sex? How can you avoid that situation?

8. Are there more questions about puberty and sex that you are not clear about? Do you feel comfortable talking with your parents about it? If not, who might you feel comfortable speaking with?

9. Have you made a commitment to save yourself sexually for your future wife? Why or why not?

10. Think about the last time you had an angry outburst? What do you think was really going on with your emotions?

11. What should you do when you feel angry?

Chapter 9

Red Flags

Having a thirteen-year-old in the family is like having a general-admission ticket to the movies, radio and TV.

– **Max Lerner**, American Journalist

All television is educational television. The question is: what is it teaching?

– **Nicholas Johnson**, Communications Professor

During the 1950s, John Boyd dominated fighter aviation in the U.S. Air Force. His fame came on the wings of the quirky and treacherous F-100: the infamous "Hun." Boyd was known throughout the Air Force as "Forty-Second Boyd," because he had a standing offer to all pilots that if they could defeat him in simulated air-to-air combat in under forty seconds, he would pay them $40. Like any gunslinger with a name and a reputation, he was called out many times. As an instructor at the Fighter Weapons School (FWS) at Nellis AFB, he fought students, cadre pilots, Marine and Navy pilots, and pilots from a dozen countries.

He never lost.

The myth of "Forty-Second Boyd" still rankles AF fighter pilots. They say there is no "best" pilot, that everyone has a bad day, but if they went through Nellis in the late 1950s, they knew Boyd had no bad days. And they could not come up with the name of anyone who ever defeated him.

Boyd was equally famous in the classroom where he developed the "Aerial Attack Study." Until Boyd came along, fighter pilots thought that air combat was an art rather than a science that it could never be codified. Boyd proved them wrong when he demonstrated that for every maneuver there is a series of counter maneuvers, and there is a counter to every counter. Afterwards, when fighter pilots attacked (or were attacked), they knew every option open to their adversary and how to respond.

You are about to enter a time in your life when your mind will be under attack. Our culture has created a number of ways to influence your thinking. You will see and hear things that go against God's Word. Your thinking will be challenged. There will be a number of things that will try to occupy your time. You must be prepared with counter measures. Without a guide, it will be hard to fight against the attacks. This chapter will look at the many ways culture tries to shape the way you think and act.

One of the first attacks will come from the media, and it will focus on sex. As if the testosterone racing through your body during puberty and adolescence didn't themselves provide enough sexual impulses and desires, just about everywhere you turn there are images of scantily-clad, beautiful women whose bodies and eyes seem to be saying, "I want you." Just about every TV show and movie has something about sex, whether joking about it or showcasing a sexual relationship between two unmarried people. While watching sports on television, you will see countless commercials that focus on sex. You will see commercials that tell you that if you wear this type of deodorant, girls will be all over you. You will see beautiful women advertising many products. Advertisers know what they are doing. They know what attracts the attention of boys and men. You must be very careful about what you watch and the amount of time you spend watching TV. You must also be willing to discuss what you see with your parents. Do not rely on handling the attacks on your own.

What activities do Americans do during a typical day, and how much time do they spend on each activity?

The five activities that take up the most time besides sleeping (6.1 hours) are:

1. Working (6.6 hours)

2. Watching television (3 hours)

3. Using the Internet on a home computer (2.4 hours)

4 Listening to the radio (1.7 hours)

5 Reading books (1.5 hours)

> Television can have a powerful effect on your beliefs about sex, especially beliefs about marriage and girls. The few studies done indicate that teenagers who get most of their information about sexuality from television will have higher criteria for female beauty and will accept the idea of premarital sex and extramarital intercourse with one or more partners.
>
> – UNC Center for Research in Journalism

Temptations from the media are everywhere, and the struggle to remain pure in your heart, mind and body is not an easy one, especially during the teenage years. It is a battle that too many boys lose.

What is a teenage boy to do?

1 Understand God's plan and design, as well as His standards and commands. He designed us with senses so that we might be excited by what we see and touch. He built us to see the beauty of women. He created a sex drive in us. He wants us to experience pleasure.

2 Know you are under attack. We all have a sinful nature, and our gifts are easily perverted into self-serving, sinful desires. God, being completely holy and desiring a relationship with us, calls us to a standard of perfect purity: purity of thought and action. He wants us to seek Him with all our heart, and He wants our hearts to be pure and centered on Him in the midst of a world that is not.

3 Understand God's standards are high. No sex outside of marriage. No hint of sexual immorality. No lust. No impure thoughts. Jesus tell us in Matthew 5:28 that looking lustfully at a girl is committing adultery with our hearts. That's tough.

4 Know that the battle will be difficult. We boys and men face many temptations, but perhaps none is more difficult than our struggle with sexual purity, especially pornography and the many other sins to which it leads. We boys and men are usually visual people. Things we see make a big impact on us (usually more of an impact than things girls see).

Pornography:
1. The depiction of erotic behavior (as in pictures or writing) intended to cause sexual excitement.
2. Material (as books or a photograph) that depicts erotic behavior and is intended to cause sexual excitement.
3. The depiction of acts in a sensational manner so as to arouse a quick intense emotional reaction.

– Merriam Webster's Dictionary

"Well, what's the big deal about seeing pictures and videos of naked women?" you probably wonder. Doesn't every teenage boy do it? Isn't "studying" the female body a normal and necessary part of becoming a man? "It's not like it's hurting anyone," you may think. What you may not realize, though, is that it's hurting you. First of all, any type of impurity, including sexual impurity, keeps you from enjoying intimacy with God. He doesn't reject or forsake you, but you distance yourself from Him, and you lose what He offers you in an intimate relationship with Him.

Another area of attack involves pornography. Looking at pornography changes the way men view women.

1 You can easily—and often without realizing it—start to view women as body parts.

2 You can think of them simply as sexual partners.

3 You can get a wrong impression of how women behave and of what are appropriate boundaries with them.

4 You learn to relate to women in unholy ways and in ways in which you do not have to share your own emotions and thoughts with them.

Pornography is not just a handicap for how you can relate to women. It is essentially a drug. Its images are addictive. As you look at sexually explicit images, the same chemical in your brain is being released as if you were snorting cocaine. That's powerful! This means that if you think you'll just look at porn once, you'll probably look at it often because your mind will remember it and crave it. And more than that, it can be the fuel that revs up your sexual engine so intensely that you feel a nearly irresistible urge for sexual activity with a girl or to masturbate obsessively, both of which will produce guilt.

Like the drugs we discussed a few chapters ago, a lot of teenage boys first look at pornography because of curiosity or maybe because a friend is doing it. They may think it will be an adventure; after all, it's seeking out something that is off limits—the naked female body. Some think it's a rite of passage that makes you a man. Other men feel a sense of power, strength and control when they are looking at naked women. A lot of guys are bored or feel an emptiness inside. Boys and men with a hole inside their hearts often rely on a picture or fantasy to provide the love and affirmation they aren't getting elsewhere and may feel they don't deserve. But at the end of the day, as with other drugs, pornography leads to emptiness, shame and a sense of abandonment and entrapment—things that can keep us from enjoying intimacy and joy with God.

Our sins, though forgiven through Jesus, have consequences, including long-term ones. There is a price to pay at the end of the day, even if the porn was free and seen for just a minute. Sexual impurities as a teenage boy may follow you into marriage. You may be more likely to struggle with intimacy with your wife and less likely to experience sexual fulfillment with her. You may carry guilt and images and memories you can't seem to erase. The patterns and attitudes you develop as a teenager will probably remain with you as an adult, even as a married man. You are the same person, after all. Too many boys make the mistake of thinking that what they do as a teenager doesn't matter in the long run.

What can you do to avoid getting drawn in to pornography?

1 Recognize its dangers.

2 Know it is addictive.

3 Know that millions of men once started looking at pornography, and now they can't seem to stop.

4 Know the ways it damages your thinking, your ways of relating to women and even possibly your marriage one day.

5 Know it's easier never to start than it is to stop.

6 Don't put yourself in situations where you will be tempted to see it.

7 Make the decision not to have a computer with internet access in your bedroom.

8 Have your parents put a filter on the computer and ask them to review sites you have visited.

9 Have a buddy or mentor hold you accountable for websites you hit and movies you watch.

10 Take the TV out of your room, or at least disable certain channels.

The prudent see danger and take refuge, but the simple keep going and suffer for it.

– Proverbs 27:12

You will be tempted, and you will need parents, friends and mentors to help you resist. Even one of the world's most famous and respected preachers, Billy Graham, knew he would be tempted, so he had his assistants go through his hotel room in advance and remove anything, including magazines and pictures on the wall, that could possibly lead him to impure thoughts. They removed the television. Once, with a TV that was wired in such a way that it could not be unplugged and removed, he ripped the TV out the wall and paid for the damage saying, "I'd rather pay for the damages to this hotel room, than let Satan get a stronghold in this battle and allow him to damage my soul." If Billy Graham is presented with temptations, and if Jesus faced worldly temptations in the desert, you can rest assured that you'll be tempted also.

It's not just X-rated movies and Playboy magazines and internet porn that can tempt and hurt you. The woman working out in spandex, the sexually explicit video game, the girl in a swimsuit at the pool, the bra ads in the newspaper, the Victoria Secret catalog—all these things and many others can get the male sexual engine running and off to the races. God knows how strong these temptations are and that purity doesn't come to us naturally. That's why Paul tells us in I Corinthians 6:18 to flee from them. He knows how easily they can trip us up. He knows that even a hint of sexual immorality can harm us.

Recognize that you need to train your mind just as you do your eyes. Just as your body is a reflection of what you eat, your mind is a reflection of what you see and hear. If you feed your mind junk and impurities, it will be fat and impure. There's a lot of junk food out there, but not much purity. So if you want to find that which is wholesome and pure, you have to seek it out. Keep your mind on a pure station. As the psalmist tells us in Psalms 119, having Bible verses hidden away in our hearts that we can meditate on keeps our ways pure. Paul tells us in Philippians to think about things that are true, noble, right, pure, lovely, admirable, excellent and praiseworthy. He tells us in II Corinthians 10:5 that we are to "take captive every thought to make it obedient to Christ." Clearly, our thoughts matter, and we are to be deliberate about how we regulate them.

Media Statistics Courtesy of Common Sense Media:

- Nearly two out of three TV programs contain violence, averaging six violent acts per hour.

- The average child who watches two hours of cartoons per day may see more than 10,000 violent acts a year.

- There are more than twice as many violent incidents in children's programming than in other types of programming.

- Teens who watch more than one hour of television per day are four times more likely than other teens to commit aggressive acts in adulthood.

- In a study of third and fourth graders, reducing television and video game consumption to less than one hour per day decreased verbal aggression by 50% and physical aggression by 40%.

- According to the American Academy of Pediatrics, violence is a leading cause of death for children, adolescents, and young adults—more prevalent than disease, cancer, or congenital disorders.

- By the time kids enter middle school, they will have seen 8,000 murders and 100,000 more acts of violence on broadcast television alone.

- Younger kids are particularly vulnerable to the health effects of media violence—especially those under seven who can't easily distinguish between fantasy and reality.

- The younger kids are when they see a violent or scary movie or TV show, the longer-lasting the effects—particularly in nightmares and increased anxiety.

Another attack from our culture deals with the music you listen to. We listen to music for a number of reasons. We listen to relax, to divert our attention from stressful situations and for enjoyment. Many boys use music as a way to express themselves. We look to musical artists as role models. In today's society, many varieties of music have lyrics that talk about issues involving violence and sex. These may include heavy metal, rock, rap and alternative music. Let's be clear, not all music is bad. In fact, many artists use their music to empower people. Many lyrics talk about social and religious issues that need to be addressed. Other lyrics talk about general topics and are just fun to listen to. During the last decade we have seen music lyrics become more and more violent and sexually explicit. Experts argue that this can cause problems in children and adolescents. Studies show that the average teenager listens to approximately forty hours of music in a given week. One is to assume that somewhere in the mix a child is going to hear something derogatory or objectionable, as it has become the norm in today's society. The challenge for you will be to recognize that objectionable material and keep it out of your playlist. Do not assume that because a song has a good beat or rhythm it makes the lyrics appropriate. Music can be very deceiving. Be on your guard and listen carefully to the message the lyrics are giving you. Be willing to find new music if you have to.

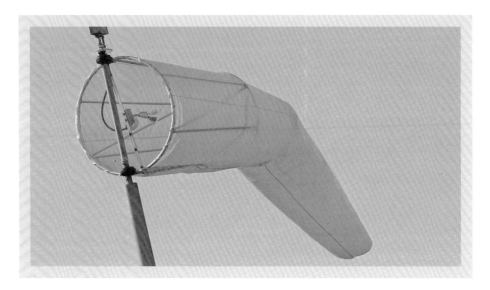

You should also look carefully at what movies you choose to watch. Everyone loves going to the movies. In fact, over the next few years, the movie theater might become a regular spot for you and your friends. Knowing this, you should be extremely careful in your movie selections. Just because your parents, friends, or the movie industry think a movie is acceptable for you does not mean that it is automatically a good decision for you to watch it. There are certain movies you should avoid. Your movie selections matter. Many movies give you an incorrect picture of what sex, marriage and relationships look like. Sometimes you might assume that just because these famous actors say it or do it that it is automatically right. That is not the case. Once again we must stress that not every movie is bad. In fact, many movies have positive messages. The struggle for you in the upcoming years will be to make wise decisions on what you should or should not watch.

If you are currently struggling with any of these issues, seek God's forgiveness and help. Ask for Him to give you the strength to walk away from it. It's an amazing thing to be forgiven and to have His aid. If you have impure images or thoughts from the past that you can't seem to shake, you may need to be very disciplined in meditating on verses and wholesome songs and other things to replace the old ones. A parent or counselor may also be able to help you. Many men need help with all of this. Address it now before it grows into a bigger problem.

Don't buy into the fake manhood that part of our culture is trying to sell. It offers a false sense of adventure, instead of authentic and bold ones that real men should be pursuing. It keeps us from being true friends because it limits our ability to be open and intimate. We don't protect and serve girls and women, as noble knights and servant leaders should, when we are selfishly using them in ways to satisfy our own lusts. Most significantly, it turns our hearts from God as we seek to find our value in something cheap and sinful rather than gaining our worth through His creation and redemption of us. Don't choose to cheat yourself out of authentic manhood and the fullness of joy and fellowship with your Creator.

Chapter 9
Questions for Reflection and Discussion

1. Why do so many boys and men struggle with the temptation of pornography? Is it a struggle you have already faced?

2. How does pornography hurt you?

3. In what ways is pornography like a drug?

4. How can you lessen the likelihood that you will be enticed by pornography?

5. What hints of sexual immorality are near you? What can you do to get rid of them? What specific things do you need to train your eyes to bounce off of?

6. Do you have a friend or mentor who will hold you accountable in your effort to be pure? If not, who would be someone you could ask?

7. Read and think about the lyrics of your three favorite songs. What sort of messages about women and sex do they contain? Are they consistent with the Biblical view of women and sex? Do you need to get some new music?

8. What are the last five movies you've seen? What about the last five TV shows? Are they corrupting your image of girls and women? What shows and movies are out right now that you may be tempted to see but know you should not?

9. What are you doing to train your mind to think about those things that are pure and admirable and noble and excellent?

Chapter 10

Call Signs And Crew Chiefs

You don't choose your family. They are God's gift to you, as you are to them.

      – Bishop Desmond Tutu

I mean, I look at my dad. He was twenty when he started having a family, and he was always the coolest dad. He did everything for his kids, and he never made us feel like he was pressured. I know that it must be a great feeling to be a guy like that.

      – Adam Sandler, Actor and Comedian

During a peacekeeping mission over Bosnia, Air Force pilot Captain Scott O'Grady was shot down in enemy territory. Undetected, he survived by sleeping under camouflage netting during the day and moving at night. Capt. O'Grady avoided patrolling Serbs until he made contact with NATO forces six days later. Military leadership debated who would lead the rescue, and chose the 24th Marine Expeditionary Unit (Special Operations Capable) to conduct a TRAP (Tactical Recovery of Aircraft and Personnel) mission. The unit was chosen for its rapid deployment capabilities and extensive training prior to the assignment.

After pulling O'Grady aboard their helicopter and flying low to the ground, the unit dodged two shoulder-launched surface-to-air missiles. Forty-five minutes later, they landed safely on USS Kearsarge. Captain O' Grady survived many ups and downs during his six days in enemy territory. He experienced fear and relief. He used every piece of training he received in order to survive. Even though that time was extremely different for him, his perseverance and training gave him the opportunity to survive. In the end, Captain O' Grady had to rely on the help of others to get him out of a difficult situation. The same might be said for you and your relationship with your family. At some point, you will be faced with a difficult situation in your life and you will need the help of others. The first place you should turn is your family.

If there is one thing in your life that is given to you without any input from you it is your family. You didn't choose them. Though you didn't choose them, you belong to your family forever, even though they quite possibly will be the greatest source in your life of heartaches and headaches, struggles and stresses, trials and tragedies, conflicts and collisions. Without a doubt, they can cause you to lose sleep or even, it might seem at times, to lose your sanity. But your family also can be one of the greatest sources of relief and respect, happiness and healing, and laughter and love you will ever experience. Knowing how to interact better with your family can be of great value to you, especially during the teenage years when how you relate to them, and how you understand them, are changing.

Dr. Tim Kimmel, in his book *Raising Kids for True Greatness*, tells of ten ways to be a great member of their family.

1 Everybody helps everybody… always, in whatever ways are needed.

2 Be upbeat, positive and encouraging.

3 Remember, "please" and "thank you" are not just good manners; they're the calling cards of a grateful heart.

4 Have a lot of fun, just not at the expense of anyone else.

5 Each week, do your best to eat as many meals as possible together as a family.

6 Respect one another's space and stuff.

7 Guard family traditions, and do your best to celebrate all birthdays, holidays and major milestones.

8 Guard the morals and integrity of everyone around you.

9 Be quick to rally around a family member who is down, whether it's a result of sickness, injury, failure, rejection or discouragement.

10 Assume that the Lord Jesus is a participant in every detail of your family.

Most teenagers experience more stresses and conflicts with their parents than they did as children. The sources of these problems are many, but they often include feeling like your parents are treating you like a child when you are a teenager. Part of growing up is becoming independent, and it is natural, to some extent, to resist when parents and other adults try to impose what seem to be child-like structures on us when we are not children. It's normal to start to develop your own ideas and preferences—ideas and preferences that may be different from those of your mom and dad. This is a key step in establishing your own identity—the main task of adolescence.

You can't control what your parents will do, but you can control your own attitudes, words and behaviors, and if you follow the principles in this chapter, we think it is much more likely that you and your parents will get along well and that they will generally provide you with the latitude you need and want.

Right off, you should understand that God ordains the family unit. He provides families that they might protect, teach and help you prosper. No matter how much your parents or siblings might drive you crazy, no matter how deeply they might disappoint or pain you sometimes, we feel certain that you are better off because you are growing up in a family unit, even if in a divorced, single-parent or blended family.

Family Principles to Live By:

- Be respectful of your family.
- Be grateful for your family.
- Know that every family, and every individual, is flawed.

The first, and most important principle, comes across very directly in the Bible. It is to honor and obey your parents. Both the Old and New Testaments stress this, and it is the first commandment with a promise. "Honor your father and your mother, as the Lord your God has commanded you, so that you may live long and that it may go well with you in the land the Lord your God is giving you (Deuteronomy 5:16)."

What does it mean to honor your parents?

- It means to listen carefully to them and to obey them.
- It means to be respectful to them in what you say to them and how you say it to them.
- No back-talking or defiance.
- No excuses or delays.
- No sarcasm.
- It is immediate obedience, preferably with a "sir" or "ma'am."
- Keep your tone and body language positive.

♣ Your obedience to them, unless it is contrary to God's Word or an appropriate civil law, is not conditional on your liking what they are telling you to do. It is based simply on the fact that they are your parents and God tells us to honor them.

It's a smart thing to obey them because they are wiser than you are. Sure, they are probably out of touch with teen culture and clueless about some things, just as you will be one day as a parent. Sure, they are probably hypocrites sometimes and make their share of mistakes, but that doesn't mean they aren't wise. They've seen and experienced first hand a lot of things you haven't. They know what your blind-spots are; they know where certain paths lead and how things usually turn out. They love you fiercely and want what is best for you, and it is in setting rules and boundaries, and even in disciplining you, that a parent most deeply conveys his or her love for you. It is not by being a buddy to you, nor is it by trying to make you happy or give you everything you want. So accept and respect their rules, and their discipline, by seeing them as love. One day, you'll be grateful for the boundaries and rules they set; you'll see how that structure helped you to succeed and how their discipline sharpened your character. As crazy as it sounds now, you will even be glad they said no and grounded you.

Your relationship with them, though, is not just a one-way street of your obedience. It depends on your ability to communicate openly and often with your parents so they can understand you. The responsibility is on you to make sure your parents understand what is happening with you. They can't read your mind, know what you are feeling or know what you need if you don't tell them. Tell them about the pressures you are feeling from them or your friends, your need for some space, that a friend is not being a friend, that you wish they came to more of your games or didn't seem too busy for you. Many parents back away from asking their teenage sons about what is on their hearts, about their needs and struggles and the important things in life. Or they ask at times or in ways that are uncomfortable to teenage boys. So the burden for good communication about both the big and little things in your life falls with you.

If you are taking the initiative to communicate openly and often with your parents, it is likely that you are helping to build their trust of you. And your parents' trust of you will make a huge difference in your relationship with them and your teenage years.

There is a simple formula: the more your parents trust you, the more freedom you will get. Here are some ideas about earning trust from your parents:

1. Always be honest with your parents.

2. If there was drinking at a party, tell them.

3. If you failed a math test, let them know.

4. You can never lose their love by mistakes you make (no matter how great), but you can lose their trust by being dishonest.

5. Once you have lost their trust, it will put a strain on your relationship with them, and they will probably restrict some things you would like to do. And it will take time to earn their trust again.

6. Demonstrate responsibility.

Responsibility shows that you are growing up and maturing and can handle bigger things. Consciously or subconsciously, they will view you as older and may grant you some of the privileges that accompany it. Doing dishes, mowing the yard, watching and playing with your younger siblings and other acts of service can yield more than allowance. Take the initiative to do those things without being asked; you might be surprised to see what you parents give you without your asking.

Things Not to Do When it Comes to Family:

♣ Don't measure their love of you by the material things they give—or don't give—you. Parents have differing financial resources, but even if they could give you everything you wanted, it would be unfortunate and unwise if they did. You would almost certainly feel entitled, become spoiled and place too much emphasis on your possessions at the expense of your soul.

♣ Don't think their love depends on your performance. Even though they may cheer loudly for you, praise and brag about your accomplishments and push you (maybe too much) to achieve and show disappointment when you don't achieve as much, don't think your successes and failures have any bearing on their love for you. If you are feeling that their love depends on your performance—or if you are feeling a lot of pressure from them—take the initiative to tell them.

♣ Don't try to divide and conquer or get one parent to overrule a decision the other has made. It's manipulative and immature to do this, and if you act in childish ways like this, it shouldn't surprise you if they treat you like a child.

♣ Don't write off your parents' needs and wants. Your mom and dad are more than simply your parents, even though that is almost exclusively how you see them. They are individuals with their own personalities, passions and dreams. They have ups and downs, failures and frustrations. They get tired and stressed at their jobs and at home. They have friends who sometimes hurt or disappoint them. They care about how people view them. They want to prosper and like to be affirmed and encouraged. They have the same basic needs and wants you do.

♣ Don't retreat too far and too often from your family because you are wired for connection and intimacy. You need that time and closeness with your family. If you retreat too frequently to your headphones and bedroom and the internet, you'll miss out on the relationships needed for your well-being, as well as memories you will one day laugh about and even cherish.

It's easy for sons and daughters to forget these things about their parents, and when you forget these things, you aren't going to be giving them the sort of love and encouragement that they crave. Take the initiative to figure out creative ways to tell them—and to demonstrate to them—that you love them.

Creative Ways to Show Your Love and Respect to Your Parents:

1 Write an occasional letter to tell them you love them or are proud of them.

2 Make them a dinner and clean up the kitchen for them.

3 Clean out the garage.

4 Give them a night out while you watch your younger sibling.

5 Demonstrate the Golden Rule to them—treating them the way you want to be treated.

Of course, a family is more than just parents. Brothers and sisters can fill your house with noise and chaos and conflicts. They, like you, have good and bad days, differing needs and wants, and the more people who live together, the more chances there are for you to be buffeted by the ups and downs of others and the more you may have to compete for the attention and affection of your parents.

Ten Ways to Be a Great Big Brother:

1 Be kind. Remember the old saying, "you can catch more bees with honey than you can with vinegar?" Ok, well even if you don't, niceness cuts down on tension. Try it.

2 Be a sibling, not a parent. Telling them to stay out of your CDs probably won't work. Chances are it will be more effective coming from Mom or Dad.

3 Give them some space. Sure, they can be annoying. But guess what? You can be, too. Everyone needs room to breathe.

4 Spend five minutes. Just spending a few minutes a day talking to them about something...anything, from a dream you had last night to what shirt you should wear today. They'll be psyched to share their opinions and you'll see that every conversation doesn't have to end in a fight.

5 Spend more than five minutes. Once you've gotten the five-minute thing down, set aside some real time to spend with them. Play a board game, or take them to a movie you'd never go see without them.

6 Let them tag along...sometimes. Take them with you when you are not going to be doing anything strictly for teenagers, like maybe going to get something to eat. They'll feel included and cool 'cause they get to hang with you.

7 Set an example. You may argue, and you may call each other names, but when it comes down to it, they look up to you.

8 Use your skills. Practice basketball or soccer with them. Teach your brother or sister how to throw, catch or ride a bike.

9 Teach them. Homework can be hard, and usually your parents are left to help them with it, late at night after a hard days work. You know how to help them and make it fun, too.

10 No younger siblings? You can still be a great brother or sister to a kid in need of a mentor!

If you have siblings, your relationship with them is important. As children created, like you in the image of God, they are due respect and dignity from you, of course. 1 Timothy 5:8 tells us we are to protect and nurture younger siblings. Be a noble knight. As a man, you are to look after the needs of all your siblings. You are to practice the Golden Rule with them, just as you should with your parents. It's not always easy to do these things. Jealousy can get in the way, like it did with Cain who killed his brother Abel and with Joseph's brothers who sold him into slavery. Maybe your sister is making better grades than you are, or your brother is a better athlete. Maybe your dad seems to spend more time with your little brother than you, or your sister always seems to get better presents. Maybe you can't ever get on the computer because of them, or they nag or tattle or pick at you until it drives you crazy. Do not let arguments or jealousy put a strain on your relationship with your brother or sister.

Once upon a time two brothers, who lived on adjoining farms, fell into conflict. It was the first serious rift in forty years of farming side by side, sharing machinery and trading labor and goods as needed. Then the long collaboration fell apart. It began with a small misunderstanding, and it grew into a major difference. Finally, it exploded into an exchange of bitter words followed by weeks of silence.

One morning there was a knock on John's door. He opened it to find a man with a carpenter's tool box. "I'm looking for a few days' work," he said. "Perhaps you would have a few small jobs here and there I could help with? Could I help you?" "Yes," said the older brother. "I do have a job for you."

"Look across the creek at that farm. That's my neighbor; in fact, it's my younger brother. Last week there was a meadow between us and he took his bulldozer to the river levee and now there is a creek between us. Well, he may have done this to spite me, but I'll do him one better."

"See that pile of lumber by the barn? I want you to build me a fence—an eight-foot fence—so I won't need to see his place or his face anymore."

The carpenter said, "I think I understand the situation. Show me the nails and the post-hole digger, and I'll be able to do a job that pleases you."

The older brother had to go to town, so he helped the carpenter get the materials ready, and then he was off for the day. The carpenter worked hard all that day measuring, sawing, nailing. About sunset when the farmer returned, the carpenter had just finished his job.

The farmer's eyes opened wide, his jaw dropped. There was no fence there at all. It was a bridge—a bridge stretching from one side of the creek to the other! A fine piece of work, handrails and all—and the neighbor, his younger brother, was coming toward them, his hand outstretched. "You are quite a fellow to build this bridge after all I've said and done." The two brothers stood at each end of the bridge, and then they met in the middle, taking each other's hand.

The family is the gymnasium which God uses to strengthen your ability to be compassionate and tolerant and loving and forgiving. If you lived in a family that didn't test you, you wouldn't be growing. You wouldn't have as many opportunities to develop the attitude of a true friend; you wouldn't have as many chances to serve. So be grateful that He's growing you through your siblings and parents and the struggles you are facing, and remember the love and respect they are due.

One other thing: if you can demonstrate the maturity to rise above the typical arguments and pettiness in families, your parents will probably view you as more mature and therefore probably give you more of the freedom you are craving. Ask God to give you the patience to endure the inevitable conflicts and chaos that all families have, and pray for your parents and siblings. You may be surprised at how praying changes your feelings for your family and how you relate with them.

You will, during the teenage years, feel a lot of different emotions about your family. If you live in a family in which your parents are divorced, separated and/or remarried (about half of marriages end in divorce), your emotions toward your family may be more complicated at times and intense at other times. Although you are not responsible for your parents and anything relating to their marriage, their choices and actions have a big impact on you. Unfortunately and unfairly, marriage difficulties and changes can create confusion, worry, depression and anger among children.

For most children and teenagers whose parents have separated or divorced, they have three key questions that cause much anxiety:

- First, they wonder if they have done something to cause the breakdown of the marriage. "Is it my fault?" the boy wonders, as guilt consumes him.

- Second, he wonders what he can do to get them back together, and he feels pressure to do this and frustration and despair when he can't.

- Third, he wonders what his life will be like after the divorce. Expect to wrestle with those questions, but, more importantly, know the answers. You did not do anything to cause the divorce, there is nothing you can do to get them back together and your life will be different in various ways (but you can adjust and lead a great life).

Children of divorced parents face some unique tensions and issues to sort out:

- They can feel embarrassment and shame and certainly confusion and sometimes anger or loneliness.

- They have to deal with the grief of not getting to spend as much time with a parent (usually the dad), and they often feel a loss of security that the family provided.

- They often feel divided loyalties between their mom and dad and that they are being pulled between the two of them, or being pulled between two households or between their old family and a new blended family with step-siblings or half-siblings.

- They need to learn how to share things with new siblings, including the time and attention of a parent.

- They have to adjust to new rules and personalities. In blended families, they can feel like they have to choose between loving their dad or step-dad, or their mom or step-mom.

- They have to still figure out how to honor and obey their parents—and forgive them. It's a lot of tough things to deal with during the already-challenging season of adolescence.

While you will experience pain and various emotions, there are a few things you can do that often helpful to boys in situations like this. First, ask to have an active role in making decisions about the arrangements of your schedule concerning time and details with your parents. Tell them what days and hours you prefer and think make sense for how you divide your time. Similarly, request family meetings or family counseling to discuss tensions and problems the split or blended family is having. Studies have found that children who can have an active say in these things have a more positive experience and a more positive outlook than children who do not. Also, ask the questions of your parents that are on your mind. In most cases, children are not given full explanations and a chance to ask questions, and this can lead to confusion and questions that never get closure or answered.

Having someone you can talk to about these family hurts, questions and tensions is also very important. Most commonly, children talk to a friend or a grandparent. Seeing a professional counselor, either at school or elsewhere, can be very helpful to give you perspective, encouragement and some ideas for how best to handle this. Don't be too cool to seek help in these very complicated situations. Don't be afraid to share with a classmate what you are feeling, and if you know of a classmate whose parents are going through a divorce, take the initiative to reach out to him. It's a time to demonstrate true friendship, even if he's not a close friend at the time.

As we conclude this chapter on families, we have a few thoughts about fathers. Boys around their adolescent years especially crave time with their fathers. Ideally, each of you has a dad who is able to give you the time and attention you want and need. Unfortunately, a lot of dads are very busy, or they don't live with their sons, or there is just not the closeness that boys and dads want, or dads aren't sure if their sons want to talk about certain delicate and possibly awkward topics. We encourage you, if at all possible, to take it upon yourself to ask your dad to spend special, one-on-one time with you. Ask him if, one night a month, just the two of you can go out to dinner or some activity. Ask him if the two of you can take a trip together once a year.

Rick was born in 1962 to Dick and Judy Hoyt. As a result of oxygen deprivation to Rick's brain at the time of his birth, Rick was diagnosed as a spastic quadriplegic with cerebral palsy. Dick and Judy were advised to institutionalize Rick because there was no chance of him recovering, and little hope for Rick to live a "normal" life. This was just the beginning of Dick and Judy's quest for Rick's inclusion in community, sports, education and one day, the workplace.

In the spring of 1977, Rick told his father that he wanted to participate in a five-mile benefit run for a Lacrosse player who had been paralyzed in an accident. Far from being a long-distance runner, Dick agreed to push Rick in his wheelchair and they finished all five miles, coming in next to last. That night, Rick told his father, "Dad, when I'm running, it feels like I'm not handicapped."

This realization was just the beginning of what would become over 1,000 races completed, including marathons, duathlons and triathlons (six of them being Ironman competitions). Also adding to their list of achievements, Dick and Rick biked and ran across the U.S. in 1992, completing a full 3,735 miles in forty five days.

In a triathlon, Dick will pull Rick in a boat with a bungee cord attached to a vest around his waist and to the front of the boat for the swimming stage. For the biking stage, Rick will ride a special two-seater bicycle, and then Dick will push Rick in his custom made running chair (for the running stage).

Rick was once asked, if he could give his father one thing, what would it be? Rick responded, "The thing I'd most like is for my dad to sit in the chair and I would push him for once."

Your dad isn't perfect—and there are probably some things about him that disappoint or annoy you, maybe even really pain you—but he's been where you are.

If the two of you will spend enough quality time together, it is likely that you will develop a relationship in which you can talk with him about anything. Having a wise man, especially your father, with whom you can share any question or struggle, and from whom you can learn about being a man, is an incredible blessing; it is also, unfortunately, an uncommon one, for even most fathers and sons don't talk often and freely about the most important things in life. Ask your dad about his boyhood and his relationship with his father. Ask him about girls and women and the different topics in this book. Ask him to read and discuss this book with you. Ask him about God. Ask him what it means to be a man.

Chapter 10
Questions for Reflection and Discussion

1. What is causing you the most stress with your parents? Are there things your parents just don't seem to understand about you? Have you talked with them about it?

2. Do you have a regular time that you and your parents talk about your life and relationship?

3. Are you showing honor to your parents? What can you do this week to show them honor?

4. Why should you not expect or want your parents to treat you as an equal or friend? Why should you not want them to give you everything you want?

5. Are you doing anything on a regular basis in your family to demonstrate responsibility and maturity? If not, what could you do this week?

6. Have you violated your parents' trust? What can you tell them about that would show them that you will be truthful in letting them know about things you could possibly keep hidden from them?

7. What can you do that would meet a real need or desire of one or both your parents?

8. How are you treating your siblings? What are you doing to protect them? Do you pray regularly for them?

9. What do you think God is trying to teach you from the difficulties you face with your family?

10. If you are living in a divorced, single-parent or blended family, are you talking to anyone about the unique struggles that you are facing? If not, who could you be talking to?

11. Are you getting to spend enough quality time with your parents, especially your dad? If not, what can you ask them or him to do with you?

Chapter 11

Flight School

When I was in high school, I earned the pimple award and every other gross-out award.

— Jack Nicholson, Actor

Even in high school I was very interested in history – why people do the things they do. As a kid I spent a lot of time trying to relate the past to the present.

— George Lucas, Filmmaker

A significant milestone specific to the fighter pilot is attending the centrifuge, a dastardly little machine made famous by its amusement park portrayals in various movies. The centrifuge is not nearly as fun to actually experience. Much as the movies show, pilots are seat-belted into a cubicle that simulates a cockpit on the end of a long arm that spins at amazing speeds, compressing the pilots under increased gravity (G) forces.

Future F-16 pilots are required to stay conscious under a force of nine Gs for ten seconds, which is admittedly no small feat. In fact, sustaining Gs in the centrifuge is significantly more difficult than in the actual aircraft and is extremely physically demanding. Though sometimes the object of scorn and derision for the pain it causes its victims (both physically, for those that endure it, and emotionally for those whose career paths change as a result of it), the training and experience of the centrifuge undoubtedly save lives. Fighter pilots fly high-performance aircraft, and without the proper training, they would be more likely to G-LOC (Gravity induced Loss Of Consciousness). There are many "hard tests" that fighter pilots and military officers must endure in order to progress. Those who desire to succeed must pay attention to their training, persevere through the challenge, learn from the experience, and then reach back and help those who will follow after them. Your upcoming years of school will be quite the same. You will need to endure in order to progress. Your school years will require you to pay attention, persevere and learn as much as possible.

Let's be honest for a moment. School isn't always the greatest. It's a drag sometimes. Sometimes it's stressful. Sometimes it's boring. You probably prefer Saturdays and the summer to school. But it's the law that you be in school through most of your teenage years, so your dreaming of a school free life is just a dream.

Since you have to be in school, and given that you will spend as many or more of your waking hours at school than even at home, it's a good idea to make it as positive an experience as possible. Like many things in life, your attitude toward things often determines your experience with them. In other words, if you can develop a positive attitude toward school, you will be far more likely to actually enjoy it. In the same way, if you have a bad attitude toward school, you will probably dislike school. Learning to control your attitude is a very important skill to develop. There is a great saying that attitude determines altitude—in other words, how you think about things determines how high you go or how low you stay. In his book, *Strengthening The Grip*, Charles Swindoll writes that life is 10% what happens and 90% how we respond to it.

A man came across three masons who were working at chipping chunks of granite from large blocks. The first seemed unhappy at his job, chipping away and frequently looking at his watch. When the man asked what it was that he was doing, the first mason responded rather curtly, "I'm hammering this stupid rock, and I can't wait 'til five when I can go home."

A second mason, seemingly more interested in his work, was hammering diligently, and when asked what it was that he was doing, answered, "Well, I'm molding this block of rock so that it can be used with others to construct a wall. It's not bad work, but I'll sure be glad when it's done." A third mason was hammering at his block fervently, taking time to stand back and admire his work. He chipped off small pieces until he was satisfied that it was the best he could do. When he was questioned about his work he stopped, gazed skyward and proudly proclaimed, "I...am building a cathedral." Three men, three different attitudes, all doing the same job.

In this chapter, we'll try to give you a perspective on school that can possibly change your attitude toward it, as well as some principles to guide you at school and some practical things to do and not do.

First of all, God created everything about you, including your mind. As you learn more about the brain as you get older, it will probably boggle your mind as you realize just how complex and incredible it is. God wants you to use your mind. He tells us in Mark 12:30 and Luke 10:27 that He wants you to love Him with all of your mind. He designed you to think, reason and understand. He designed you to explore, and He created a world and universe worthy to be discovered and explored. The grandeur, size, diversity and complexity of the universe and the world are powerful invitations to use our minds. Our mind is a gift meant to be used and enjoyed, not put away in a closet or on a dusty shelf. We have found that the more we learn about the world—the smarter we get—the more it leads us to God.

My philosophy of life is that if we make up our mind what we are going to make of our lives, then work hard toward that goal, we never lose – somehow we win out.

– Ronald Reagan, Former President

To use your mind well takes training. It doesn't happen automatically or without work. Major league baseball players have spent thousands of hours in the batting cage. They have studied pitchers. They have lifted weights. They have fielded ground balls, learned to throw a curve ball and been taught where to hit the ball in different situations. They have listened to their coaches. They have played pressure-filled games. They didn't just show up one day at Yankee Stadium because they wanted to play Major League Baseball.

It's the same way with your mind. It needs training. You need to exercise it so it doesn't become flabby, soft and underdeveloped. You need people who can teach you. You need a place where you can go regularly to exercise your mind. You need a mental batting cage or workout room. Such a place exists. It's called school.

Ideally, school would be a place that is always intellectually stimulating. You would develop a thirst to learn about the world and its history. Science and math would excite you. Ideas and art and music would stir something in your soul. Your school experience would deepen the way you understand yourself. Ideally, school would be a place of excitement and passion.

School, unfortunately, is sometimes boring. It can sometimes seem that what you are learning is irrelevant—that is has no connection to your life and doesn't seem like it will be of any value in the future. "After all, what can Greek philosophers and gerunds and geometric theorems have to do with my life?" you may wonder. In the course of your school career, you will ask that question about things you are studying.

What do you do when school seems mundane, boring and without much purpose?

- You work hard anyway.
- You stay dedicated.
- You do what you are supposed to do.
- You do everything to the best of your ability.

There are, though, some things you can do that may make school more interesting for you. You can approach it with the mindset that you will make it an adventure. Remember, real men are adventurers. They create adventures. How can you do this at school? Read more than what is assigned in areas that interest you. If you are bored in math but love airplanes, read about them, and you may see how math and physics are an important part of how a plane flies. You may see math in a fresh way. If your brief study of World War II seems interesting, go on-line, research and read first-hand accounts from veterans, or view video clips from bombing raids. It may make a textbook come alive.

Microsoft co-founder and chief executive officer Bill Gates has become the wealthiest man in America and one of the most influential personalities in the ever-evolving computer industry. He was the second child and only son of William Henry Gates Jr., a successful Seattle attorney, and Mary Maxwell, a former schoolteacher. Kristi, his older sister, later became his tax accountant and Libby, his younger sister, lives in Seattle raising her two children. Gates enjoyed a normal, active childhood and participated in sports, joined the Cub Scouts and spent summers with his family in Bremerton, Washington.

Although Gates's parents had a law career in mind for their son, he developed an early interest in computer science and began studying computers in the seventh grade at Seattle's Lakeside School. Lakeside was a private school chosen by Gates's parents in the hopes that it would be more challenging for their son's intellectual drive and curiosity. At Lakeside, Gates came to know Paul Allen, a classmate with similar interests in technology who would eventually become his business partner. Immediately, Gates and Allen realized the potential of the young computer industry. They made learning an adventure, doing more than just the basics of school.

In your classes, ask tough questions of your teachers. School is for your learning—not simply for your listening. As long as you are respectful, it's ok to disagree with a teacher or what the textbook says. The mark of a mature student is one who can think for himself, not just memorize what a teacher or textbook says. Forming your own opinions and beliefs, and understanding how arguments are crafted and conclusions are reached, can make school more exciting and relevant. Also, try to figure out how different subjects might fit together. Can you take an idea from a novel you are reading in English and apply it to something in history? How does math express scientific laws? What is the relationship between science and faith? Thinking in your mind about questions like that can, sometimes, make classes more interesting and even adventuresome. So can seeking out people with different backgrounds and interests from your own. If you are white, make a point to ask an African-American classmate how he views the Civil War or the Civil Rights movement. You'll learn that we all see and experience the world, including school, differently. Also, learn about religions and faith traditions different from your own.

If you do these things, we think that school will be more exciting for you. You may even find parts of it enjoyable and stimulating, but parts of it may still be slow at times, and there is good that comes even from that. God builds our character in mundane tasks. Doing your best in unexciting things builds self-discipline. It teaches you to persevere, not to quit, and not to cut corners or take short-cuts. It builds a strong work ethic. You develop a reputation as someone who is faithful, hard-working and dependable. If you develop those skills and characteristics, along with that reputation, you will be given more responsibilities, opportunities and occasions for leadership. Those skills will come in handy one day in ways that you might not be able to imagine right now, in ways probably necessary to execute a heroic purpose for your life. You'll probably look back at that boring time and realize that you learned important lessons.

Florida basketball coach Billy Donovan's attitude plan:

 Always making today my best day.

 Taking pride in a job well done.

 Treating others with respect.

 Isolating my negative thoughts.

 Treating tasks as opportunities.

 Utilizing my talents every day.

 Doing the job right the first time.

 Expecting positive outcomes daily.

 Speaking well of others every day.

 Many athletes have tremendous God–given gifts, but they don't focus on the development of those gifts. Who are these individuals? You've never heard of them—and you never will. It's true in sports and it's true everywhere in life. Hard work is the difference. Very hard work.

– John Wooden, Hall of Fame Basketball Coach

You should also work hard in school because how you perform in school will have a big impact on the trajectory of your future schooling and career. Students who make good grades are actively involved, and good citizens are much more likely to have more choices when it comes to picking future schools they want to attend. Many high school seniors, as they start applying to colleges, regret that their earlier school performances will keep them from being admitted to schools they now wish they could attend. Whether it's college or graduate school, those schools will each look at how you performed in school. They will want to see whether or not you showed dedication, a good work ethic and curiosity about learning in many different subjects. They will want to know how you were involved in activities at school. They will want to know what sort of a citizen you were.

When you finish your schooling and start seeking employment, you will be asked once again about how—and what—you did at school. And once again, those individuals who were faithful and responsible at school will have a big advantage in being offered more opportunities than those who did not. Know that how you do in school now will make more of a difference in the future than you probably realize.

Although how you do in school matters, and you should always do your best, be careful not to define yourself by what you do or achieve at school. We boys and men have a tendency to think that what we achieve shows who we are. It's one of the myths of manhood. You are not a math grade or an honor roll student. You are not a lacrosse champion or musician. You are not a boyfriend of a terrific girl. You may achieve those things, or those things may be a part of your life, but that is not who you are.

Don't Make Good Things the Ultimate Things:

- Your belief that you have to perform can lead to anxiety and possible depression if you fall short.
- They can lead to arrogance when you sometimes achieve important things, but it will ultimately lead to confusion and despair when you realize that they don't give your life meaning.

If you can learn the crucial lesson now that grades and games and girls should not consume or define your life, then you will be more likely to avoid the performance pressures that hold many men hostage.

You can also relieve yourself of stress by not comparing yourself to your classmates. God created you differently than He did your classmate who sits next to you in history class. Some people have greater intellectual abilities than other people do. Some have bodies that incline them to be faster or stronger. Some people are wired to be especially talented at art or hear music differently. We have differing personalities and looks and styles. We men are usually wired to be competitive and make comparisons. It can be a fine and appropriate thing to compete, but don't let the results of your competition define you or how you think about yourself. Resist the temptation to compare yourself. Be the best you can be. Make the best grades you can, whatever they are. If you can let go of comparisons, your school years will be better ones.

It hurt me a great deal. It put a lot of pressure on me because I was at a young age and the writers around here and throughout the league started comparing me to Cobb. It put a lot of pressure on me.

– Al Kaline, Hall of Fame Outfielder

You will also have a more positive schooling experience if you don't over-schedule yourself. Too many teenagers get involved in too many activities. They end up tired and stressed and not doing anything as well as they should. Schoolwork suffers. So do self-esteem, relationships and health. As a general rule of thumb, we think you should limit yourself to one significant extracurricular activity at a time. If you swim competitively on your school's team or on a team outside your school, don't act in a play at the same time. Pick one activity per season, and commit your best efforts to it. Learn to say no to things that will over-commit you or compromise your well-being and health.

Possible Effects of Doing Too Much:

1. You will be too tired to complete your homework or chores around the house.

2. You will miss out on opportunities for unstructured free play, things that all boys need.

3. You will become too focused on competition.

4. You will miss opportunities for family fun.

5. You will miss out on opportunities to serve others in the community.

Be mindful of maintaining a healthy diet and getting the proper amount of sleep. To be at your best, you need to eat well and sleep at least nine hours a night. Most teenagers get too much junk food and too little sleep, and it has a big impact. Even when you are sleeping, your brain is at work. It is sorting and storing information, replacing chemicals and solving problems. When you don't sleep enough, your brain doesn't fully do those things, and therefore it is difficult to concentrate, read and solve problems. You can't remember things as well, perform as well or run as fast. Your immune system doesn't work as well, so you will get sick more often. You are more likely to be grumpy and irritable. You are more likely to get in argument. In short, you short-change yourself, as a student and as a friend to others.

Developing Good Study Habits:

- Have a regular plan, a schedule for when and how you will accomplish that amount of work.
- Make sure you have a quiet place without distractions. For many teenagers, the telephone, TV and computer prevent sustained and significant study. You should study in a place without any of those things. You may be amazed at how much you can get done without distractions.
- Let your friends and family members know of your homework schedule and ask them to respect and support your time without their distracting you. It is possible to carve out significant study time and still maintain a reasonable amount of time each week for connecting with friends, including a girlfriend.

Of course, school is about a lot more than just classes and studies, even though that is the purpose and most important part of it. It is a training ground for your approaching manhood. It is a place of tests—not simply the academic ones, but ones of virtue and character.

Are you up to the challenge?

- Will you be a true friend?
- Will your friendships be based on your desire for popularity and coolness, or will they be based on deep emotional ties and sacrifices?
- Can you let go of shallow friendships and wait for true ones?

- ♟ Will you develop and exercise the skills of the noble knight by defending the reputation of your classmates and girls and by respecting your teachers and rules and authority, even when you may not like them?

- ♟ Will you be a moral motivator at your school by treating all of your classmates, especially those who seem most different from you, with respect and dignity and fairness and inclusion?

- ♟ Will you discourage bullying?

- ♟ Will you serve your school by contributing your time and talent to make it a better place for others, or will you only take from your school and only participate in those things that bring you success and enjoyment?

- ♟ Will you be willing to fail a math test because you have the integrity to pass the test of honor by not cheating?

Real men have integrity: they act the same way when no one is looking, and they are the same person at school as they are at home as they are at church as they are with their friends.

Several years ago, there was a story about Reuben Gonzolas who was in the final match of his first professional racquetball tournament. He was playing the perennial champion for his first shot at a victory on the pro circuit. At match point in the fifth and final game, Gonzolas made a super "kill shot" into the front corner to win the tournament. The referee called it good, and one of the linemen confirmed the shot was a winner.

But after a moment's hesitation, Gonzolas turned and declared that his shot had skipped into the wall, hitting the floor first. As a result, the serve went to his opponent, who went on to win the match.

Reuben Gonzolas walked off the court; everyone was stunned. The next issue of a leading racquetball magazine featured Gonzolas on its cover. The lead editorial searched and questioned for an explanation for the first ever occurrence on the professional racquetball circuit. Who could ever imagine it in any sport or endeavor? Here was a player with everything officially in his favor, with victory in his grasp, who disqualifies himself at match point and loses.

When asked why he did it, Gonzolas replied, "It was the only thing I could do to maintain my integrity."

There will be difficult tests and hard times in school for you and everyone else. There will be pressure and uncertainty and fear for everyone. There will be periodic failures and setbacks. Know that your teachers and administrators care about you, even if they don't always understand or appreciate your music or teenage culture. Seek out a teacher or counselor in whom you can confide and seek advice. Don't be too cool or tough to get the help you need. We adults know that school can be tough, and that being a teenager is often hard. Schools are places not simply of learning, but of leaning. Learn to lean on adults and on your family. More importantly, learn to lean on God.

Chapter 11
Questions for Reflection and Discussion

1. What should you do when school seems boring? What may God be trying to teach you through things that don't excite you?

2. What subject or topic really excites you? What can you do to dig in and learn more about it?

3. Does how you do in school really impact your future?

4. Are you trying to achieve for the right reasons? What are the right—and wrong—reasons to achieve?

5. Are you stressed at school? If so, why? What do you think are some of the most common causes of stress at school?

6. How many hours have you slept for each of the last seven nights? Are you sleeping enough? If not, what changes do you need to make, or what discipline do you need to develop?

7. What are you doing to serve your school to make it a better place? What can you do to demonstrate servant leadership this month at your school?

8. What can you do to show respect and dignity to all of your classmates, especially those who are most different from you?

9. Is there someone at your school—a teacher, counselor, coach or administrator—whom you would feel comfortable talking to about struggles and challenges you may encounter?

Chapter 12

Medals Of Honor

Success is a lousy teacher. It seduces smart people into thinking they can't lose.

— **Bill Gates**, Microsoft Founder

Money has never made man happy, nor will it; there is nothing in its nature to produce happiness. The more of it one has the more one wants.

— **Benjamin Franklin**, One of the USA Founding Fathers

Captain Johnny Ferrier, a pilot for the famed Blue Angles, shreds across the blue sky. Onlookers at the national air show notice smoke billowing from the back of his Navy jet. On the radio, his superior pleads for Johnny to save his life. "Bail out, Johnny, Bail out! You've still got time!" His superior shouts through the receiver. But Johnny doesn't make his move. He knows that if he bails, thousands of innocent bystanders will lose their lives in the crash.

"Bail out!" his superior tries again. Nothing. The stress of the G-force only allows Johnny to answer his superior by blowing three puffs of smoke, just to let him know that he was alright—that he was under control. The crowd watches in amazement as Johnny courageously steers his plane to the only place not occupied by people. A small meadow is where Johnny makes his final statement to the world.

Captain Johnny Ferrier's statement was one of ultimate honor for the people down below him. His courage to take his own life, for the lives of others, might be hard for people to understand, especially in light of Johnny's beautiful young wife and children he left behind. However, the card his wife found tucked away in his wallet the day of his death explains why he gave his own life. It simply read, "God first, others second, and myself third." Success in the mind of Captain Ferrier was different from what our culture teaches us. He was willing to give up the things of this world for the glory of God and the good of others.

There was a pretty popular song that came out many years ago entitled "Don't Worry, Be Happy." The singer, Bobby McFerrin, looked so happy and relaxed. His song is about what so many of us think is the goal of life—to be happy—and what we spend most of our lives pursuing. After all, The U.S. Constitution guarantees the pursuit of happiness.

Let's be honest. It's nice to be happy. You're happy when your school is called off for a snow day, when you pitch a shut-out in your baseball game, when you hear that cute girl likes you, when everyone says what a great guy you are, when summer finally arrives, when your friends are really nice to you, when your dad spends a lot of time with you, when people think you're cool, when your favorite football team wins, when you go to the beach, when you get awesome presents, when the sky is blue and when there's no homework.

The problem with happiness, though, is that it is based on circumstances beyond your control. You can't make the weather be sunny or your friends be nice to you. You can't control if your pro football team wins or loses any more than you can control if that girl likes you. You can't make it be summer all year. Your teachers will decide on homework regardless of your wishes. Happiness depends on other people and things that you cannot control, so it eventually lets you down.

Why, then, do we pursue happiness so intently if it's only going to disappoint us? Ever since humans fell when Adam and Eve first sinned in the Garden of Eden, we have been cut off from God. In the core of our deepest being, we are sinful, broken and lonely, and we live in a fallen, messed-up world. We therefore have a hole in our hearts. The hole in our hearts, and the loneliness we experience, don't feel good, so we naturally seek things that will make us feel better. Happiness makes us feel better, but it is sort of like taking a Tylenol to cure cancer. It might make you feel better, sometimes, for a while, but it doesn't actually do anything to eradicate the disease.

But our purpose in life is not to be happy. Pursuing happiness is a dead end. Making happiness your #1 goal is a way to guarantee yourself disappointment and then despair, because happiness depends on the people and things of this world which also are broken. Trying to fill an emptiness in your life with happiness is like giving a deaf man a pair of glasses so he can hear. It's the wrong solution. We'll talk about the right solution in a minute, but first, we'll look at the brother of happiness—success.

I've failed over and over and over again in my life and that is why I succeed.

– Michael Jordan, NBA Hall of Fame Guard

If happiness is the wrong solution on which to base our life, then what about working to be successful? After all, can't we control how hard we work, and if we work hard enough and do the right things, shouldn't we be successful? Isn't it a good thing to be successful, and won't our success somehow make our life valuable and therefore fill that hole we have in our hearts? Besides, doesn't it feel good to be successful?

Again, let's be honest. We boys and men especially like success. We strive to be successful. Winning is more fun than losing, whether playing paint-ball, laser-tag or a soccer game. We prefer to get A's rather than C's, to make the game-winning shot rather than miss it. It feels good to be recognized in front of the school for winning a chess tournament or having your artwork chosen to be displayed at school. There is a satisfaction that comes with completing a task successfully. We aspire to be leaders, to make the honor roll, to be the best, to win, to go to the best schools we can, to get the best jobs we can and to be president of the company. In short, we like to be successful, and we like it when other people know we are successful.

If you are like many other boys, you probably have some or all of your trophies, medals, ribbons and awards placed carefully somewhere in your room. They are reminders of your triumphs, your victories, your excellence and your successes. You probably look at them from time to time and think about what you did to earn them. You may know exactly how many of them you have.

John Wooden has widely been regarded as the best college basketball coach in history. He was the first person ever to be enshrined in The Basketball Hall of Fame as both a player and a coach, and his ten NCAA championships at UCLA have never been matched. The keys to his success in motivating and inspiring his players are the same principles that make one's life a success. His players have said that they don't recall Coach Wooden ever stressing the importance of winning a game. For him, it was about sticking to the fundamentals.

On the first day of practice at the beginning of a new season, he would say to his players that he wasn't going to talk to them about winning or losing because that was a by-product of preparation. He preferred to focus on the process of having them become the best team they were capable of becoming. Even when he taught English in high school, he recalled seeing parents criticize their children for receiving less than an A or B. He wanted to communicate the message that success in life isn't just about how much possessions you have or how powerful you've become; it's about finding peace of mind in knowing you are the best that you can be.

The problem with success, like happiness, is that we make it the purpose of our life when in fact it is not. We make good things the ultimate things. Like happiness, success will let you down because you aren't good enough to succeed all the time. You'll miss shots and do the wrong thing. You'll be too tired sometimes to succeed. Others will beat you. Sometimes, your sinful nature will keep you from doing all of the right things to succeed.

Not only will success let you down, but having to succeed puts a lot of pressure on you—too much pressure in fact.

Where can this pressure come from?

- Your parents
- Yourself
- Friends
- Teammates

Although it's a dead end like happiness is, many teenage boys and men are addicted to success. Many of them get a taste of it, and they need more and more and more, even if they are not achieving the success they want. And even for those teenagers and men who seem so successful by how we usually judge success, they can easily start to define themselves by their successes.

For teenage boys, their identity is often wrapped up in things like the following:

- Grades
- Wins and losses
- Girlfriends
- Number of friends
- Athletic ability

For men, their identity is often wrapped up in things like the following:

- Title at work
- Bank account
- Possessions

Especially for boys and men, we get caught up so quickly in believing that who we are is a reflection of what we do. So we learn to work hard and put intense pressure on ourselves to perform for others and ourselves. We think we have to perform for God the way we do for other people and ourselves, and we end up putting our trust in ourselves rather than in Him. Many people in today's culture label this as idolatry. When we make something in our life more important than our relationship with God, it becomes an idol.

When you look to some created thing to give you what only God can give you that is idolatry. An idol is anything in your life that is so central to your life that you can't have a meaningful life if you lose it.

– Dr. Tim Keller, Pastor of Redeemer Presbyterian Church, New York

An idol can be anything:

- Family
- Career
- Making money
- Achievement
- Fame
- Physical beauty
- Social standing
- Romantic relationships
- Skill
- Political or social cause
- Good behavior
- Religious or church activity

Each and every day, we have an important choice to make. Will we worship the things of this world or the things of God? Our thoughts and minds should be totally consumed with bringing glory to God in all we say and do. Think about the first few words of our manhood definition: a real man glorifies God. That is your purpose in life. No matter where you are or what you have, your purpose remains the same: to live your life for the glory of God. Your relationship with Jesus Christ must be the most important thing in your life. This relationship is the only way to win the battle against the pressures of this world.

One of those potential idols is money. It can also be called materialism. Oil tycoon J. Paul Getty once said, "The best things in life are things." According to author C.J. Mahaney, "Materialism is fundamentally a focus on and a trust in what we can touch and possess." Money is the primary way we obtain such things. You can see how these things go together. Materialism is not just having too many possessions. Owning a lot of possessions in itself is not bad. It only becomes a problem when we link who we are with what we have. It is a heart issue.

No servant can serve two masters, for either he will hate the one and love the other, or he will be devoted to the one and despise the other. You cannot serve God and money.

– Luke 16:13

On November 26, 1922, Howard Carter made archaeological history by unearthing the tomb of King Tutankhamen. It was an extraordinary discovery made more remarkable because the tomb still contained most of its treasures. Filling the burial chamber were dismantled chariots, gilded figures, thrones—everything a king would need to support him in the afterlife. But Tut was a fool. He thought he could keep the possessions that mattered to him. Wrong. King Tut left the building, yet his treasures remain. It's perpetually on tour now like a 70s classic rock band.

-from the book Worldliness by C.J. Mahaney

Be Careful of materialism during the teenage years!

- ♣ You will probably care more about what you wear and what you have than before.
- ♣ You may want many of the things your friends have.
- ♣ You may think you will be more popular if you have more things, especially the latest and coolest items.
- ♣ You may think you are simply the sum of what you have.
- ♣ You may think that money can buy everything.

So now we've met three things competing for your heart: happiness, success and money. Most boys your age and men know them all very well, even if they wish they had more of these things and base their lives on them; they think that they are the purpose of life. This mistake is probably the main reason that so many men today feel very confused and empty, have so many mid-life crises and feel such a profound sense of doubt and despair deep in their souls. Ever since they were boys, they've been told to climb a certain mountain—the mountain of happiness, success and money. They've worked hard to climb the mountain. They've been very tired and stressed for much of the climb, but they've learned the skills of the hiker and rock-climber and have performed all of the best moves with all of the best gear. But as they get to the top, up above the clouds, they realize that they've been climbing the wrong mountain. In the distance, they see a mountain that is far grander than the one they have been climbing for years: a mountain they didn't know existed. What do they do? As they are wondering why no one told them they had set out for the wrong mountain, they feel a rumble beneath their feet. They start to wonder if their mountain is starting to crumble.

God has a different mountain for you to climb. In fact, He'll do the hard part for you. God tells us there is a different purpose for your life, and He has a different plan for it. It's simple and yet radical, the reverse of what you would expect. Compared to what the world says, it's upside down and inside out. That's how different it is.

Let's look at God's plan for us.

God says that man's purpose—his chief end—is to glorify God and to enjoy Him forever. Your purpose is to do things that bring Him honor: things that praise Him, things that tell Him you know how powerful and good He is, things that demonstrate to others that you know and love the Lord. In short, it is to worship Him each day in all parts of our lives. God loves us to worship Him (not just in church, but by how we act on Friday nights, how we think about and treat girls, how we use our money and positions and opportunities).

What Your Purpose is Not!

- ✦ To be happy or successful.
- ✦ To be the best athlete.
- ✦ To attend the most prestigious college.
- ✦ To be comfortable.
- ✦ To live in a certain size house in a particular neighborhood.
- ✦ To have a pretty wife.
- ✦ To have successful children.

The second part of our purpose is to enjoy Him. God is full of love. Out of His love, He has given us a beautiful world, and He has endowed us with many talents, gifts and opportunities. Joy and happiness are very different. Happiness, as we saw earlier, depends on your circumstances that you can't control and that will change. Joy, on the other hand, is based on what God, who is unchanging, has done for you. It is based on knowing with both your head and your heart that God loves you and values you in a way that is much deeper and more profound than anyone on earth does. It is knowing that your sins of yesterday, today and tomorrow are forgotten and forgiven because Jesus took them on for you on the cross.

The life God has in mind for us is not boring. Remember our manhood definition explains that God calls us to a life adventure.

- He'll give you significance rather than just success.
- You will see that your life has meaning and value.
- He will help you to see how you can make a difference with your friends, at your school and in your communities.

Many men realize, usually late in their lives, that all of their achievements, jobs, money and so forth no longer mean much to them. They seem insignificant and cheap, even if they worked hard or paid a lot to get them. They realize that their successes did not give their life significance.

Realizing that your possessions and success will not give you significance frees you to develop a heroic purpose for your life—something that is big and grand and will be deeply rewarding, something a lot bigger than a grade or admission to a school with a certain reputation. Realizing that your belongings and success will not give you significance frees you up to live as a bold adventurer—to seek out opportunities and challenges that truly matter and make you feel truly alive. It frees you up from feeling like you can only work in professions that pay a lot of money; it gives you freedom to work with the poor, to teach, to be missionaries, to be a doctor in the inner-city or a third world country.

Living in God's purpose for your life does something else very powerful. It takes pressure off you. And pressure is something that most teenage boys and then men struggle with because we place too much value on success. It's hard to walk around thinking that who you are as a person depends on the grades you make, the games you win, the college you get into and the progression with which you are promoted at work. While you should work hard, hold high standards, set goals and do your best, you should be very careful to make sure that you aren't doing them because you feel the need to perform and succeed. God tells us to take our value and worth from Him. He assures us of His love and that we were created in His image. We were not created in the image of a straight-A student or CEO or great guitarist or championship golfer. We don't have to perform for Him. We don't have to make certain grades from Him to love us. We don't have to lead a company to get to heaven. We can't earn or perform our way to heaven. Instead, we can relax because God has already done all of that for us. God's sacrifice of His Son Jesus on the cross is sufficient for us to get to heaven, if we simply accept that gift.

Relax!

+ Enjoy the fact that God's done the work already for you.
+ Let go of the need to perform and be perfect.
+ Let go of the guilt when you fall short.
+ Don't be afraid to fail.

Living in God's purpose for your life also changes the way you think about—and use—money and your material possessions. We live in the most affluent country in the history of the world, and everywhere we turn, we are hit with images of the good life. Advertisers spend billions of dollars each year to convince us that their product is the ticket to a better, happier, more successful or healthier life. TV shows, magazines and movies portray images of the good life as well and the idea that the more you have, the better you are.

The Bible, which has about 2,350 verses concerning money, presents a different view of money and material possessions. It's radical and unexpected, but it's wise and Godly. In a nutshell, it is this: be very, very careful with money. It is very dangerous because its use is very easily perverted. Remember, one of Satan's favorite tricks is to take something good and pervert it. Here are some of the things the Bible says about money and our belongings:

+ The love of money is the root of all evil.
+ Our stuff will rust and rot and be worthless.
+ Our money will not save us.
+ Our money can easily become our idol that we worship instead of God.

♣   Having a lot of money often leads to forgetting about the needs of others and not making moral and just decisions for the rest of the community.

♣   Our money can easily makes us selfish and greedy.

♣   It often leads to immorality and arrogance about ourselves.

Money gives us a false sense of security. We think it brings happiness, but it doesn't. Research has shown that although as a country we are about twice as rich as we were fifty years ago, we are less happy than before. Though America is the richest country in the world, Americans are not the happiest people—not by a long shot. Studies of people who have won the lottery show that many of them end up depressed, confused and paranoid. Money can also bring an arrogance, an unwholesome view of power and a false sense that rules don't apply or that you can perhaps buy your way out of the consequences for poor decisions.

Money is a good thing if it is used properly. There is nothing wrong with having money, and if your family has a lot of it, or if one day you have a lot of it, be thankful, but be careful. Be very careful. Our friend, Sandy Willson, Second Presbyterian Church Senior Pastor, has said that you should make sure that you make money your servant, not your master. Don't let it control you. Don't let it lull you into thinking that just because you can buy most anything, you are entitled to most anything. Know that some things—the most important things in life—are priceless, just like the MasterCard commercials say. The sooner you start to see how privileges like money are potential pitfalls, the wiser you will be. If you can learn now to see the shortcomings of possessions and money, you will be much more likely to lead a life of great significance and purpose later.

Warren Buffett, seventy five, the world's second-richest man according to *Fortune Magazine*, is worth $44 billion. Buffett will donate 85% of his fortune amassed from stock in the Berkshire Hathaway company to five foundations. The donations, which will come from Buffett's Berkshire Hathaway shares, amount to about $37 billion. Mellody Hobson, *Good Morning America's* financial contributor and president of Ariel Capital Management, said Buffett's act of generosity was a defining moment in the history of business and philanthropy. Bill Gates and Buffett share the philosophy that giving your children too much money is a burden, not a gift, and is not a rational thing to do with all that wealth. Seven years ago, Buffett told ABC News' *Nightline* that being born into wealth did not entitle his children to fortune.

"Buffett once told *Fortune Magazine*: 'A very rich person would leave his kids enough to do anything, but not enough to do nothing,'" Hobson said. "He says he and his wife talked about it and decided they shouldn't pass huge amounts of money along to their children. They believe their kids were born with the advantages of wealth, and grew up with great opportunities because of that. He says they had a gigantic head start, and that dynastic megawealth would further tilt the playing field in America, when we should be trying to make it more level." Buffett is rich, observers say, but he has simple tastes and a simple philosophy. "The money has never meant much to him," Loomis said. "He still lives in the same house he lived in forty years ago. He just is not interested in spending a lot of money."

-story courtesy of ABC news

All of this is, of course, easier said than done. Most people are consumed with the pursuit of happiness, success and money. It usually begins in late childhood and really takes off in the teenage years. Most teenage boys develop an intense drive to perform and achieve—one that gathers more momentum in manhood. Most teenage boys and men have a great fear of failure. Often, that fear of failure motivates us even more than succeeding.

Check out this short resume of Abraham Lincoln, one of our country's greatest presidents.

- In 1831, he suffered a business failure.
- In 1832, he was defeated in a bid for the state legislature.
- In 1833, he underwent a second business failure.
- In 1835, his fiancé died.
- In 1836, he experienced a mental breakdown.
- In 1838, he was defeated for speaker of the state legislature.
- In 1840, he was defeated for the office of elector.
- In 1843, he was defeated for land officer.

- ♣ In 1846, he won an election for the Congress.
- ♣ In 1848, he was defeated in his reelection bid.
- ♣ In 1855, he was defeated in a run for the Senate.
- ♣ In 1856, he was defeated in his bid for vice president.
- ♣ In 1858, he lost again in another attempt at the Senate.
- ♣ In 1860, he was elected President of the United States.

Look at the failures that many of the heroes of the Bible experienced. Adam and Eve had everything in the world and blew it. Abraham failed in having children for most of his life. Moses killed a man and he never got into the Promised Land. Job lost his family, wealth and health. Jonah defied God. Peter denied knowing Jesus. Paul killed lots of Christians.

Consider it pure joy, my brothers, whenever you face trials of many kinds, because you know that the testing of your faith develops perseverance. Perseverance must finish its work so that you may be mature and complete, not lacking anything.

– James 1:2-4

Tough times:

- ♣ Build our faith.
- ♣ Reveal our hearts.
- ♣ Forge our character.

In the upcoming years, each of you will experience pain, hardship and failures. Your friends will disappoint and hurt you and sometimes desert you. A girl will break your heart. A loved one will die. You'll embarrass yourself and doubt yourself. You'll bomb a test, drop the big pass, and get rejection letters from colleges. You'll make big and little mistakes and commit a host of sins. Your sins and mistakes are opportunities to experience the sweet grace and forgiveness of God. As weird as this sounds, be grateful for times like these because you'll be a better person for them. Know that it's healthy to fail and not get everything you want; it reminds us that God's purpose for our life is bigger and better—and sometimes different—than our own goals.

If you know the sort of man that God wants you to be—if you are living out His purpose for your life—you'll navigate your way through the minefield of failures and hardships a lot more easily and quickly than if you don't have that perspective. If you haven't made happiness, success and money the goal of your life, then you'll experience much more balance, joy and purpose in your life than your classmates who are so driven to perform and achieve and impress.

The apostle Paul had a great perspective on happiness, success and money. He was a powerful, wealthy and respected man who had the finest education and the best things. He was successful, but he realized that something was missing from life. He ended up spending part of his life in prison, and it was there that he wrote this to his friends in Philippi.

"I have learned to be content whatever the circumstances. I know what it is to be in need, and I know what it is to have plenty. I have learned the secret of being content in any and every situation, whether well-fed or hungry, whether living in plenty or in want. I can do everything through him who gives me strength."

We hope you set your mind not on the usual stuff of the teenage years, and not on the usual things of manhood—popularity, possessions, positions and power. Don't let these things become your idols. Don't start climbing the wrong mountain.

The way is not by performance or success, but by humility and surrender. Set aside your manly ego—and the myth that men have to be strong and successful on their own—and admit to God you can't do it yourself. Give your heart to Christ. Get on the operating table, be a heart patient, give up control and ask God to perform surgery—to give you the new heart He promises. It will change your life, your teenage years and your manhood.

Chapter 12

Questions for Reflection and Discussion

1. What makes you really happy? Is it something you can control and count on?

2. What do you think the difference is between happiness and joy? If you could just have one, which one would you want and why?

3. How does the world define success? How does God define success? Are they the same?

4. What are your idols? What are the things in your life that it would be very difficult to be without?

5. What are the dangers and downsides of riches?

6. Are you using some of your allowance or money to help and serve others? If not, what could you start doing?

7. Are there things you are trusting in that could let you down?

8. What has been one of your biggest failures? What do you think God was teaching you? Did you grow?

9. What is the purpose of life? Are your goals aligned with God's goals?

Chapter 13

Final Tune Up

Twenty years from now you will be more disappointed by the things you didn't do than by the ones you did do. So throw off the bowlines. Sail away from the safe harbor. Catch the trade winds in your sails. Explore. Dream. Discover.

— **Mark Twain**, Author

I firmly believe that any man's finest hour, the greatest fulfillment of all that he holds dear, is that moment when he has worked his heart out in a good cause and lies exhausted on the field of battle— victorious.

— **Uince Lombardi**, Hall of Fame Coach

Chuck Yeager was not born with a silver spoon in his mouth. He grew up in a small town in West Virginia as one of five children. His family lived for a time in a three room house in which Chuck and his brother slept in the living room on a pull-out couch. His mom cooked cornmeal mush for breakfast, with the leftovers from that meal being fried up and served for dinner. The idea of Chuck going to college was never even considered.

Instead, when the boy turned eighteen, he joined the US Army Air Corps as an airplane mechanic. When the opportunity came up, he applied to become a "Flying Sargent." Once he was accepted, he found himself in a position he would remain in his whole career—the odd man out. Almost all the other men were college graduates who would become commissioned officers.

At first Yeager was intimidated by his well-educated peers, worried he would not be able to keep up. But in the air the men were "all created equal," and Yeager's humble background gave him skills that compensated for his lack of a degree and quickly moved him to the head of the pack.

Everyone agrees that one of the qualities that made Yeager into a legendary pilot was his exceptional eyes. With 20/10 vision, he could see tiny specks fifty miles away from the cockpit. He saw the enemy coming long before anyone else did.

From his dad, he picked up a love and aptitude for engineering and mechanical skills. His father was a natural gas driller and would take Chuck out into the field to fix machinery and shoot wells. His father also taught him how to take apart and put back together an engine. This hands-on training gave Yeager a passion for understanding absolutely everything about how planes worked and a leg up on the competition. Being a test pilot was a dangerous and deadly career; little mistakes and oversights left dozens of pilots dead. There was no room for error.

So Yeager wanted to know everything he could about every single plane he flew. He pored over the manual, studied the plane's parts and asked question after question of the flight engineers. When something went wrong at 800 mph, Yeager knew how to address it and what decision to make. He became one with the machine; he knew his plane like a cowboy knows his horse.

We hope that you take this book and read over it again and again like Chuck Yeager did with his plane manuals. In reading this book, we hope you've gotten a clearer sense of what it means to be a man and an idea of some of the challenges you will be facing in the upcoming years. The teenage years are an exciting time of growing independence and exploration, new passions and possibilities. They are years when you are establishing your self-identity, including your beliefs and values. It is a very important time in your life!

We hope that our definition of manhood sticks with you for the rest of your life.

Manhood- A real man glorifies God by seeking an adventuresome life of purpose and passion as he protects and serves others.

We pray that your life will be lived to the glory of God and marked by seven virtues:

 The True Friend: Leave No Man Behind

 The Humble Hero: Develop A God Sized Vision

 The Servant Leader: I Am Third

 The Moral Motivator: Make A Difference

 The Bold Adventurer: Don't Sit Around

 The Noble Knight: Called To Duty

 The Heart Patient: Give Up Control

God designed you to live a fulfilling and purposeful life as a teenager and a man. Your choices make a difference in the life you lead and experience. Realizing the purpose and fulfillment God has in mind for you depends not simply on following certain advice and rules, though that's part of it. The most important thing is developing a personal relationship with God. It is experiencing fellowship with Him and the fullness of His love. It is having a heart for the Lord. God wants your heart more than merely your words or behavior.

The principle runs through all life from top to bottom. Give up yourself, and you will find your real self. Lose your life and you'll save it. Submit to death, death of your ambitions and favorite wishes every day and death of your whole body in the end: submit with every fiber of your being, and you will find eternal life. Keep nothing back. Nothing that you have not given away will ever be really yours. Nothing in you that has not died will ever be raised from the dead. Look for yourself, and you will find in the long run only hatred, loneliness, despair, rage, ruin, and decay. But look for Christ and you will find Him, and with Him everything else thrown in.

– C.S.Lewis, from Beyond Personality

In this final chapter, we will issue a challenge. We will ask you questions and we want you to answer them honestly. This will be the only way you can truly see where you are on the path to authentic manhood. As you read this chapter, take an honest look back and see whether you are prepared to take on this mission. The flight plan has been issued. It is up to you to get in the seat and let God take control of your journey.

Challenge 1

Are you willing to make a complete commitment?

You are committed to a number of things right now. Some guys are committed to sports. Others are committed to art or music. While those are all good things, being completely committed to becoming a Godly man is far more important. The journey to real, authentic manhood is not easy. It will require you to make decisions that might not be the most popular. It will force you to take a stand even when nobody else is willing. Becoming a godly man requires complete commitment. Are you willing to make that commitment?

Are you willing-

 To be a True Friend and leave no man behind?

 To be a Humble Hero and develop a God-sized vision for your life?

 To be a Servant Leader and put yourself third?

 To be a Moral Motivator and make a difference in the world?

 To be a Bold Adventurer and not sit around?

 To be a Noble Knight and accept your call to duty?

 To be a Heart Patient and give up control?

One day in 1860, a great crowd assembled at Niagara Falls to see the famous tightrope walker Blondin cross the falls. Blondin would attempt to walk over 1000 feet on a wire that stretched from the American side of the falls to the Canadian side. After walking across the falls, Blondin decided to do something more exciting. He would attempt to push a wheelbarrow across the same wire. The crowd assembled for this daring feat was excited to see if the great tightrope walker could accomplish this difficult feat. Before he began, Blondin asked the crowd if they believed he could take a person across in the wheelbarrow. They all shouted, "We believe, we believe!" He then asked the crowd if anyone was willing to get in and allow him to push them across. No one accepted the offer. Finally, Blondin's manager and closest friend got in and received the ride of his life. It took complete commitment for that man to ride across the falls under someone else's control. God calls us to that same commitment. The call to Godly manhood is a call to commitment. We are to surrender our lives to God and live our lives in service to Him. The journey might be scary, but there is no doubt that it will be the ride of your life. Real men are willing to get in the wheelbarrow and allow God to push them through this journey. It requires complete commitment.

Challenge 2

Will you be unaffected by outside influences?

There are many things in this world that want your attention. Commercials want you to buy a certain product. Websites want you to use their services. Magazines draw your attention by placing good-looking women on the cover. The more time you spend watching, reading or listening to something, the more effect it will have on your life. The journey to manhood is no different. You cannot allow the world's view of manhood to shape your thinking. According to the Barna Research Group, the average Christian spends about ten minutes per day with God. The average American spends four hours each day watching television or on the computer. What do you think is influencing you the most? The journey to Godly manhood will require you to make a commitment to spend significant time in God's Word. It will also demand that you not allow outside influences to affect your view of manhood. This is a difficult challenge. Are you willing to spend less time on selfish desires so that you can pursue the adventure God has in store for you?

Danny Wuerffel was the quarterback of the University of Florida football team and the winner of the 1996 Heisman Trophy for the nation's top college football player. As the nation's top quarterback, Danny was selected for the All-American preseason team for *Playboy* magazine. After hearing of the selection, Danny refused to pose for the team picture because of his commitment to follow Christ. He explained by making the statement, "That's not the type of person I would want to portray myself as."

Danny Wuerffel would not allow himself to be affected by outside sources. He was willing to be a Moral Motivator and make a difference. The journey to manhood will provide many opportunities for you to make decisions that will affect the rest of your life. Do not allow the temptations of the world cloud your judgment. Spend time in God's Word and allow it to shape you. This will lead you to make decisions based on the Word of God and not the ways of the world.

Challenge 3

Will you take a stand?

Becoming a Godly man will take you out of your comfort zone. In other words, it will not be easy. Real, authentic manhood seeks to live a life to the glory of God. Sometimes it is not popular with others. It might cause you to lose friends. Your status and reputation might not be what it used to be, but the path to Godly manhood is not intended to please men. It is intended to please God.

Your mission to become a man will force you to take a stand on certain issues. The challenge will be whether or not you are willing to do it. At the age of twenty-two, Eric Liddell was Britain's greatest hope for a gold medal in the 100 meter race. When Eric received the 1924 Olympic Games race schedule, he refused to run because the event was to be held on Sunday. The idea of racing on the "Lord's Day" was unthinkable for Eric because he had made a decision long before to rest from work and sports and to honor God on Sundays. Many of his countrymen considered him a traitor for refusing to run, and newspapers criticized him for his decision. But Eric would not compromise his commitment and instead began preparing for the 400 meters, a race that was clearly not his strongest distance, but that wasn't on Sunday. Just before the race, one of Eric's trainers slipped him a note with a verse from the Bible that said, "He that honors me, I will honor." When the race was over, the winner and new world record holder was Eric Liddell. The earlier criticism and anger by his countrymen turned to respect and admiration, not only because he had won the gold medal for Britain, but because he was a man of uncompromising commitment to God. He was willing to take a stand even if it meant giving up a gold medal.

Those who honor me, I will honor.

– 1 Samuel 2:30

The journey to manhood will be no different. You will be tempted to take the road of success and popularity in place of respect and admiration. We challenge you to take the road that God calls us all men to. This is the road that seeks to glorify and honor God in all you do. This road calls us to be a Heart Patient and give up control of our lives. Are you willing to "let go and let God" take control of your life?

The challenge has been issued. The question is, "Are you ready to accept it?" The good news is that we do not have to go on this journey alone. God has given us parents, friends and mentors to help us navigate the journey. Do not hesitate to seek out the help of others who have gone through this journey before you. They will be a valuable resource to you. Begin to surround yourself with True Friends who journey with you. Never go through this journey alone. Gather your true friends and make a commitment to each other. This will be extremely helpful as you begin this journey. The road is long and it helps to have traveling companions.

The good news of God's Word gives us encouragement as well. God promises us we will find Him if we truly seek Him. He promises us His Holy Spirit to empower and direct and comfort us. He promises us new hearts and eternal salvation through His Son, Jesus Christ. He assures us we are worthy and good—the question every man eventually wrestles with. He tells us what it means to be a man. To live out the virtues of manhood will take His help. So will making the right choices about drinking and drugs and girls and getting along with your family and friends. You can't do it very well on your own. You'll figure that out one day, if you haven't already. You'll also realize that you'll go through life with a lot of guilt and despair as you fail and a lot of pressure as you to try to succeed and achieve.

God doesn't want us to be driven and motivated by guilt and fear. He wants us to receive His love, sacrifice and perfect record. But then He doesn't want us to be a passive spectator, sitting there thinking God will do everything for us.

What about you? Are you letting God work in you? Do you understand His grace and the gift He is presenting you?

The good news is that God is seeking you, and you have the opportunity—and the choice—to seek and find Him. You have the opportunity and choice to accept His gift of Jesus Christ. You have a choice to be motivated by gratitude or by guilt. You can exchange a life of achieving for receiving. You can trade in despair for joy. You can choose to be a Heart Patient and to have a heart for the Lord.

By confessing your sins and professing Jesus Christ as your Lord and Savior, you can receive His perfect record. You can experience the joy and peace that comes with knowing that, no matter what the circumstances, you are known and loved—and have a place in heaven. Knowing that frees you up to live differently—to share your love more freely, to be more adventuresome, to live purposefully and pursue passions, to serve and protect others and to create a moral society; in short, to be a better man, to be the man God designed you to be.

The mission is set before you. The plans are laid out clearly. Buckle up, it is going to be a great flight!

Appendix

A note to parents

The only thing worse than being blind is having sight but no vision.

— Helen Keller, 1880-1968

When she looked ahead, Florence Chadwick saw nothing but a solid wall of fog. Her body was numb. She had been swimming for nearly sixteen hours.

Already she was the first woman to swim the English Channel in both directions. Now, at age 34, her goal was to become the first woman to swim from Catalina Island to the California coast. On that Fourth of July morning in 1952, the sea was like an ice bath and the fog was so dense she could hardly see her support boats. Sharks cruised toward her lone figure, only to be driven away by rifle shots. Against the frigid grip of the sea, she struggled on—hour after hour—while millions watched on national television.

Alongside Florence in one of the boats, her mother and her trainer offered encouragement. They told her it wasn't much further. But all she could see was fog. They urged her not to quit. She never had…until then. With only a half mile to go, she asked to be pulled out. Still thawing her chilled body several hours later, she told a reporter, "Look, I'm not excusing myself, but if I could have seen land I might have made it." It was not fatigue or even the cold water that defeated her. It was the fog. She was unable to see her goal.

Two months later she tried again. This time, despite the same dense fog, she swam with her faith intact and her goal clearly pictured in her mind. She knew that somewhere behind that fog was land and this time she made it! Florence Chadwick became the first woman to swim the Catalina Channel, eclipsing the men's record by two hours!

The words of Florence Chadwick ring very true in our world today. We are in a battle for the hearts of our boys. The fog of the culture is thick and the journey to Godly manhood has been clouded by our culture. We need to see the shore! The goal of this book is to give you a glimpse of the shore. We want the next generation of boys to have a clear picture of what it means to be a Godly man.

Boys are too often left alone to navigate what is a very tricky and dangerous (but necessary) transition from boyhood to manhood. But even more problematic, we rarely give them a vision of where they are going. We don't tell them the sort of men they should be and what it means to be a man. We sometimes are more intentional about packing their bags for camp than we are equipping them for their emerging manhood. It is no wonder, then, that so many of them make poor choices during the teenage years and eventually join the growing numbers of men who are confused and conflicted as men, husbands and fathers.

It is our hope that this book is a resource and source of instruction and encouragement for boys, their parents, and other adults who work with boys. We write this book primarily for the boys themselves, with the aim of offering them a vision and definition of manhood before they get there, a framework for considering the challenges of adolescence and tools and strategies for making healthy and appropriate choices during those years. We hope they see the connection between the long-term vision of manhood and the short-term teenage choices. We believe that connection is vital.

We hope and think it will be helpful to them to read this just before they enter adolescence (around age 12), and then again as they are in the midst of these teenage struggles. We have sought to be relevant in covering the real issues that they will face and authentic in communicating in ways that connect with them. We encourage parents, especially dads and male mentors, to read this book alongside the boys and use it to help facilitate an open and on-going dialogue about the journey to manhood. This dialogue is one that too few parents, especially dads, have with their sons.

In developing this book, we used the Bible as our foundation. We wanted to know what God says about the sort of men He wants boys to become and how He wants them to respond to the challenges and opportunities they will face. We gleaned perspective and insights from many other sources, including some of our country's leading thinkers and researchers on male issues. Some consider the issue from a distinctly Christian perspective; others do not. Both were very important and helpful to us. We interviewed many teenage boys—and parents of teenage boys—for this book. They were invaluable in giving us a first-hand glimpse into the lives, thoughts and hearts of teenage boys. We also leaned heavily on the wisdom and experience of the talented Presbyterian Day School faculty in their great work with boys.

At the end of each chapter, we have listed some questions that we hope the boys will reflect on, write about, or ideally, discuss with their fathers, parents and/ or adult mentors.

Finally, while this book is written in light of a Christian worldview, it is our hope and belief that, regardless of the particular faith background of a boy and his parents, the book will be helpful to any boy embarking on the journey to manhood.

Braxton Brady serves as chaplain of Presbyterian Day School (PDS), a premier boys' school serving over 630 boys. A teacher, advisor and counselor to boys, Braxton is committed to helping boys grow into men of integrity and purpose. He writes and blogs frequently about how parents, especially fathers, can be intentional and strategic in training their children. Braxton and his wife, Carrie, are the parents of two sons and a daughter, and they live in Memphis.

Lee Burns serves as headmaster of Presbyterian Day School (PDS), one of America's leading boys' schools. He earned his B.A. at Dartmouth and M.Ed. at Harvard. With 20 years of teaching, administrative and mentoring experience at boys' schools, he is committed to the academic and spiritual growth of boys and young men. Lee has been a speaker at various national and international educational conferences. He lives in Memphis with his wife, Sarah, and their two sons and daughter.

Braxton Brady and **Lee Burns** are available for speaking.

For more information contact:
The Barnabas Agency
800-927-0517 EXT 110
elewis@tbbmedia.com | www.tbbmedia.com

Resources:

Promise Keepers
New Man Magazine
Men of Integrity Magazine
Focus on the Family
www.celebraterecovery.com

For more information:

info@theflightplanbook.com | www.theflightplanbook.com